Bread Machine Cookbook for Beg

Replicate The Cuisine Secrets Of Our Ancestors Thanks to the Technology

Copyright © 2023
Sarah Roslin

TABLE OF CONTENTS

1 INTRODUCTION

Making bread from scratch is time-consuming, but the results are worth it because it's nourishing and tasty. Baking bread is an involved process that needs patience, diligence, and hard labour on the part of the baker. However, it's not always necessary to do this step.

Because the bread machine does all the hard work, you can focus on the delicious results. If you're still on the fence about whether or not to purchase such a device, the recipes here should put your mind at ease. Since many people lack the patience to finish the time-consuming and labor-intensive process of making bread by hand, bread machines have become vital.

Although it is still possible to buy bread at the grocery store, baking bread at home is always a better choice because it can be tailored to the tastes and health needs of the person or family.

In the kitchen, there is a device called a bread maker that uses these ingredients to produce delicious bread. If you want to save time and effort, then getting an automatic bread machine is a great choice. An electric countertop oven specifically designed to bake loaves of bread. Tin retains its aesthetic value despite housing the electric motor, which is attached through a bottom axle. On the axle, a tiny metal paddle that is housed inside the tin rotates. The axle is held in place by a waterproof barrier that stops the bread mixture from leaking. Bread is a must for every meal, whether it be lunch, brunch, or dinner, as it has traditionally been eaten with many different types of food. Instead of purchasing bread from a store, use a bread maker.

Using a bread maker at home allows you to avoid the use of artificial substances typically seen in store-bought bread. It needs flour, water, and yeast, and you can make it better by adding things like grains and nuts. Making bread at home is usually preferable since you can tailor the recipe to your tastes and use only the freshest ingredients. If that weren't enough, there are a tonne of dirty pots and pans left over from baking traditional bread. When using a bread machine, it is necessary to add the ingredients, bake the bread, and then clean the baking pan.

Different types of bread can be created using the modern bread machine's adjustable settings. A bread maker could be useful for those who have to avoid foods like gluten because of intolerance or sensitivity. Several bread recipes are included in this book. Use only the freshest ingredients, and enjoy every delicious taste!

2 WHAT IS A BREAD MACHINE

A bread machine is a kitchen device that typically consists of a pan or bucket with a series of kneading paddles which are turned by an electric motor, and which are used to mix and knead dough into the desired consistency for baking. The shape of the pan is often cylindrical to allow rising bread dough to be pulled up the sides for faster and lighter browning.

Bread machines come in both vertical (or upright) models and horizontal models. Horizontal models are more common among home bakers.

A vertical machine generally has a single kneading paddle which is turned by an electric motor in the bottom of the pan. A horizontal version has two paddles, one on top and one on the bottom of the pan, with the top paddle turning in a clockwise direction and the bottom paddle turning counter-clockwise, to give proper kneading. In some cases, both paddles will turn in the same direction, giving a slightly harder dough and a less uniform loaf.

Some bread machines have kneading paddles that are adjustable to give different amounts of kneading based on the type of bread being made. Two tbsp or so may be added to hard rolls or chestnuts and one tbsp might be added to the soft dough used for pasta dough and meatballs. If a larger amount of kneading is required, the dough may be removed from the pan after rising for kneading in a stand mixer.

Bread machines have been a part of home kitchens for many decades. They are credited with performing several operations previously carried out by humans, including mixing ingredients, kneading and rising dough to increases its viscosity and final risen volume, allowing it to be placed in a pan and baked at a higher temperature than it would have if mixed manually or slowly by hand. They also allow the baker to prepare a loaf of bread without having to be at home for most of the preparation time.

The Bread Machine Yeast

The bread Machine Yeast is a special type of yeast that allows you to bake a variety of breads without the need for kneading or rising times. The process starts by adding the yeast and flour to your bread machine as per usual, with one exception: Instead of putting any water in the ingredients, you pour in your milk or milk substitute and let it sit at room temperature for about an hour before adding it to the dough cycle. All bread machine machines require that the yeast be dissolved in water before it can be added to the rest of the ingredients. You would have had to add it separately and wait for it to dissolve, but with bread machine yeast you can incorporate it into the dry ingredients right away. Shelf life of the bread machine yeast is indefinite if stored in its original package in a cool place.

How do yeasts function?

Yeast is a single-cell organism that reproduces and multiplies by budding, thereby creating new cells from old cells. The new cells that are produced become more numerous as they divide while the old ones are discarded. This process is called budding because each new cell breaks away from the old one. The development of yeast is vital to a successful loaf of bread. When yeast multiplies and grows, it produces carbon dioxide, which raises the temperature in the dough to encourage it to rise. When the yeast begins to die off, however, fermentation ceases and the bread becomes dry.

Contains all natural ingredients . Lab Results are guaranteed . Reliable and safe . Not artificial . FDA approved

Yeast is found naturally in most living organisms and is often used for leavening in breads, cake mixes, biscuits, muffins and other baked goods. It is a single-celled organism with a cell membrane consisting of sugar proteins. The sugar proteins that make up the yeast cells' cell membrane are largely responsible for the growth and reproduction processes of the yeast cells.

Pros and Cons of a Bread machine

Pros of Bread machine

1. It is simple to bake bread in a bread machine.

2. The process is cleaner and more straightforward than traditional bread baking.

3. Every time the bread machine produces the same consistency & exceptional taste.

4. The benefit of Jam and jelly making.

5. You don't need to do the kneading.

6. Make your fresh bread, at home, for the sandwiches.

7. You can add many ingredients to make the bread to your taste.

8. It is convenient for busy people.

9. It saves long-term resources and money.

Cons of Bread machine

1. The paddle of the machine often gets stuck in the bread, and when it is removed, a hole is caused at the end of the bread, which is a nightmare for trying to make sandwiches.

2. Some machines are limited to their pre-set program.

3. Bread machines can be fiddly to clean

4. They use a lot of electricity.

5. Most bread machines last for a limited number of loaves.

3 DIFFERENT TYPES OF BREAD MACHINES

Depending on the size of your family and your needs, you might want to purchase a different type of bread machine than what you would normally purchase. Through the use of different cycles, different machines will allow you to bake just one loaf or multiple loaves.

Little or no kneading - Many of the newer models do not require kneading at all. This is the type of bread machine you would want to purchase if you are just making bread for your family.

Knead and rise - If you need to bake a large loaf, but don't want to use your oven, this is the type of machine that you would want. Many of these machines will allow you to make up to three loaves at one time. You're likely to spend more money on this type of bread machine than others, however.

Knead, rise, and bake - This type of machine is a bit more expensive than the other types of bread machines out there but will allow you to make up to five loaves at once. Many bread machines are extremely basic and offer only a few options: kneading, mixing, and setting. They will bake the bread, but not automatically. You'll need to know what you are doing, and be able to set everything up manually. If you are just searching for a basic machine, this is probably the type that you want.

The second type of bread machine is a little bit more complex. It still offers many of the same options as a basic machine; however, you can get additional features such as delayed start time, crust color, temperature control and other things that make it easier to use than your basic machine.

This is the bread machine that most people think of when they hear the words bread machine. These machines are fully automated, and allow you to simply load your ingredients, press a button, and walk away. Many of these machines have additional features such as delayed start time, crust color, temperature control, etc., while others may only have a single button operation. These machines are some of the most expensive on the market today. This is a full-sized professional bread machine with all of the whistles and bells that you can think of . Some have automated paddle stirring and mixing, some have up to 24 hours of delay time and may even bake more than just bread. These machines are quite complex, and are usually not the best option for a home machine. They are usually the size of a large microwave oven, so make sure you have space on your kitchen counter for one of these. These machines may cost thousands of dollars, however if you are planning to bake large amounts of dough on a regular basis, then this is definitely the best option for you.

Why Do Bread Made From Bread Machine Has Similar Taste To Bread Made By Hands And Oven

There are a number of reasons why bread made with a bread machine tastes so similar to that prepared in other ways. One factor is that when yeast flakes are added to the dough, their cells rupture and combine with the starch granules to make it even more highly textured than just adding water alone. Another factor is that mechanically mixing dough gives a more even distribution of air bubbles than would be the case if it was mixed by hand.

As for why the taste, it is because flour contains a protein called gluten. This forms long chains which stretch and trap the gas formed by the yeast and also allow carbon dioxide from the yeast to dissolve in water to produce dough. When baking, these chains become firm and trap in steam, causing elasticity and expansion. Gluten is present in all flour, but the more you mix it, the more it becomes elastic.

This leads on to our final point - that of consistency. When dough is mixed by hand and baked in an oven, it will tend to come out inconsistently. The same recipe will produce different loaves each time, as the baker may not have mixed it sufficiently. It can also 'sag' in the middle, as it shrinks while cooling. Mixing it mechanically with a bread machine means that the dough can be mixed to consistent levels of elasticity and will not sag when cooling. The result is uniform in size and consistent in taste.

Different Results Between A Bread Made With Hands And A Bread Made With Bread Machine

The difference between hand-made bread and bread machine bread may not at first appear to be obvious. One may think that the ingredients are the same, as is their shape. However, if one were to take a closer look, they will see that each has different end results. If one were watching their bread dough for just a few minutes before it went into the oven, this would be apparent. The hands-baked bread is far more similar to bread that is made in a factory than the bread machine bread. The difference between the two may confuse one into thinking that they are the same product.

In order to understand this, one must look at what happens during the baking process. Bread machine dough can be very easy to manipulate, which allows for easy introduction of additives and extra ingredients into a loaf. It is also quite easy to remove ingredients from a loaf without much difficulty because of how malleable it is (Bianchi). Hand-made bread is a different story. While it can still be altered to some extent, it is far more difficult and time consuming to do so. This is why simple ingredients, such as water and flour, are most often found in hand-made bread.

As mentioned before, the hand-made bread dough has a more difficult time being manipulated than machine mix dough. This is because machine mix dough stays malleable for a long period of time than hand-made flour does. This allows for the potential of many additives and extra ingredients to be added. However, the hand-made flour is not as malleable and therefore bread that one makes from it will not have as many supplemental ingredients (Nisbet).

This give rise to the next difference between hand-made bread and bread made in a machine. Because of how malleable machine mix dough is, it can be manipulated into several shapes, which are similar to those that are found in factory produced convenience bread (Nisbet). Hand-made bread does not have the luxury of being manipulated in such away. This is because it cannot be kept malleable for long periods of time, and therefore must be baked before it becomes too firm (Nisbet). This leads to the next difference between hand-made bread and machine mix bread. The shapes of machine mix dough are much more distinct than those of hand-made dough because they are shaped into a loaf before baking. On the other hand, hand-made bread is shaped after baking because when it cools a bit, it becomes more firm and easier to manipulate (Nisbet).

This difference between hand-made bread and machine mix bread is revealed in their taste as well. Handmade bread has a distinct flavor that is one of a kind. It is because of this flavor that one must look at the other ingredients that are used in order to determine what gives it this unique taste (Nisbet). This is because each ingredient contributes something to the taste of the bread. Hand-made bread will have a distinct flavor because it uses ingredients that are simple and basic. Machine mix bread is different in this way because it contains preservatives, additives, and extra ingredients (Nisbet). These extra ingredients are what make convenience store bread so much different from hand-made.

This difference between hand-made and machine mix bread is substantial. Hand made bread is simple, natural, and comes from the ground up. Machine mix bread has been manipulated numerous times throughout its life from being initially created to being purchased in a convenience store.

4 HOW TO CLEAN A BREAD MACHINE

The first thing to do when cleaning a bread machine is to remove all of the ingredients that are required to produce the bread itself. Leaving all of these things inside will make it more difficult to clean and could get them stale. Some of these items that may be found in a typical bread machine include flour, yeast, salt, and water. When it comes to yeast, it should be save in an airtight container at room temperature out of direct sunlight and away from excessive heat. This is to ensure that it will be in good shape when the bread machine is used again. However, this yeast should not be put away for long periods of time, as it can become stale and no longer be suitable for bread making.

When there are leftover ingredients, they should be stored properly. You can do this by putting them into food-safe containers or the original container from which you took the item itself. If you place them in the original container, make sure that it is clean or emits no musty odor. If it does, you will have to clean the container before putting the ingredients in once again.

Putting all of the leftovers away is only part of cleaning a bread machine. Some residual matter can also be found on parts of the machine itself, such as inside the working chamber, on any knobs or buttons, and even along the outside where it has been stored in between uses.

You will have to properly clean all of these parts before putting the bread machine back into use. If you are sure that there are no more ingredients left in the machine, you can also place it in the dishwasher to clean it. Just make sure that it is not placed anywhere where something could fall on top of it or where someone could open it and get hurt.

When cleaning a bread machine by hand, there are additional things that you should do aside from removing all of the ingredients. Before you do anything else, ensure that the power is turned off. If the power is not off, you will just create more of a mess and risk getting hurt when you put your hand in the machine to clean it.

Next, utilize a soft sponge or cloth to wipe away any residual matter that may be on the outside. This includes crumbs from bread and other ingredients as well as anything that has gotten stuck to it or spilled on it during use. Then, you should clean the inside of the working chamber and along any seams.

To do this, place the bread machine on a flat surface. Then, fill it up with warm water that is no more than 12 inches deep. This water will help to loosen any remaining matter that is stuck on and in between the walls of the chamber. Next, add about a tbsp of lemon juice for every quart of water that you used to fill the machine. Make sure to use non-commercial lemon juice for this, as it is designed for cleaning. As you place the bread machine on a flat surface, you will notice that there is some water coming out of the bottom. This is normal and is to be expected.

After about 30 minutes of soaking, pour all of the remaining water out from the machine and drain it. Then, allow it to air dry completely before placing it back into use. Do not put it away until it is completely dry.

Be sure to clean the outside of the bread machine on a regular basis as well. You can use a damp sponge or cloth to wipe away any crumbs and residual matter. If you notice that there is water that has gotten under the knobs, you will have to unplug the machine and look under them to see if there is anything that has come loose. If there is, make sure to replace it before putting it back in use again.

Difference between a Bread Machine and a Bread Maker

Deceptively simple machines, bread makers and bread machines have been staples of the kitchen for over 50 years. If a bread maker looks like a fancy cake urn, it's usually because it was designed to make cakes in addition to bread. A single-purpose machine, on the other hand, is just that - one dedicated to its namesake task. Aside from their basic functions and designs however, there seems to be some misperception as to what distinguishes them from each other beyond the aforementioned extras.

If you're the type to read the instruction manual, you might be a little in the dark as to this, too. In fact, there aren't actually any big differences between them beyond their looks and capacities. Consider that in all likelihood, both bread machines and bread makers were created at around the same time by a product development team in some Japanese company. (There are bread makers made outside of Japan, but these are few and far between. Bread makers are primarily a Japanese invention.) They may very well have been created in the same lab and later sold separately.

A bread maker is essentially a bread machine with slightly different design choices. One of the most important design choices is the crust control setting. In most cases, a bread maker will have settings for light, medium or dark crust. A bread machine, on the other hand, will often have settings for both dark and light crust as well as a setting which controls the crust directly.

This is probably because the majority of people prefer their loaves to be evenly cooked on the inside and have a golden or brown outside - a preference which is reflected in this design feature.

Most people who buy bread makers do so because they don't have a lot of counter space. So to save space, the bread maker is designed to use less than the average bread machine. The result is an oval shaped bread maker in which the kneading paddle never leaves the top of the dough while rising. There is a special setting which bakes two smaller loaves at once, but those loaves are very small in comparison to those made by a standard bread machine.

This is a misperception which has led many to believe that bread makers aren't capable of producing a loaf of uniform size and weight, but in actuality there's nothing stopping anyone from making large loaves with a bread maker. All you should do is utilize the basic white bread setting and then add additional flour until the loaf weighs approximately 2.5 pounds when baked in a bread machine pan.

A standard bread machine is usually a rectangular white or stainless steel box with a black lid and kneading paddle. It looks like what one might imagine when they hear "bread machine." There are two kneading paddles: one on the top and another on the bottom. When the loaf is done, the paddles may be in different positions than that in which they began. This is because they rotate while mixing dough and may therefore end up at a different angle once the program is finished.Both the top and bottom paddles are capable of kneading the dough, but different programs take advantage of one or the other exclusively.

Permitted Food In A Bread Machine And Food To Avoid

Here is a list of permitted foods in a bread machine:
- Flour (All Purpose or Whole Wheat)
- Water or Milk
- Sugar
- Butter (optional)
- Salt (optional)
- Yeast (dry or fresh, depending on the type of recipe)

Food to Avoid

Keep white sugar on hand at all times if you make bread by hand – even if your recipe doesn't call for it. When you have a bread machine, there's no telling how much longer a loaf will take to bake. You may end up with a totally dried out loaf if you forget the sugar. You can also use bread machine yeast – but only if your recipe specifically calls for it. Remember, bread machine yeast is different from regular active dry yeast. It's less likely to make your bread taste bitter, but you should still be careful. If your recipe calls for regular dry yeast, you should use it instead.

Don't use too much salt in a bread machine recipe. Salt is especially important in recipes that contain other ingredients such as dried fruit or nuts, so you don't want to dilute the flavor of these ingredients by adding extra salt. We suggest varying the salt a bit between each batch of bread, so that you can control the amount of salt in each loaf.

Try to avoid using canned fruit in your bread machine recipe. After all, canned fruit is preserved with ascorbic acid, which means it won't be as sweet and juicier as fresh fruit. You may have a greater success when using fresh fruits with your machine's ingredients, but make sure to taste a few pieces before you go for it. You can then adjust the amount of fresh fruit to taste.

Don't use fresh tomatoes in an active dry yeast bread recipe. Tomato juice aids some machine recipes, but it's not necessary in these cases (where ketchup is used instead of tomato juice). Also, tomatoes contain acid that can affect the dough's rise, so you also don't want too much acidity. On the other hand, try using dried herbs such as thyme and oregano that don't contain a lot of acid.

Don't use any fruit when making a yeast bread recipe that calls for honey. Fruit and honey are a natural match made in heaven, but the yeast needs them both in order to work properly, so avoid using them together.

Frequently Asked Questions

Can i use pizza dough yeast in place of regular yeast in my bread machine?
You can utilize them in your bread machine as you would use active dry yeast. Nothing is stopping you from doing so except your conscience and knowledge of how different pizza dough yeasts are from active dry yeasts.

What distinguishes a bread machine from an oven?

An oven, a box-shaped appliance, is used to bake bread and other dishes. Due to advancements in technology, modern ovens can successfully prepare a wide range of complicated delicacies in a number of configurations. A bread machine, on the other hand, was developed solely for the purpose of producing baked goods. Place all the ingredients for making bread in the machine, and in about two to three hours, you'll have deliciously baked bread.
Can the bread machine be put in the dishwasher?
The bread machine's pan or container can be quickly cleaned in the dishwasher.

How should a home bread machine be set?

There is a user handbook that comes with a bread machine that explains how to set it up and use it without any assistance.

What Makes a Machine Bread?

A bread machine is basically a small, electrical box with a heating element, a cooling fan and an outlet for plugging in the power cord. Bread machines create baked goods by performing 3 steps which are kneading dough, rising dough to create air pockets and baking the dough.
While some people think that anything can be made in a bread machine, they are wrong. Some types of food require a lot of work which only a human cook can manage, and someone who has never tried to make a cake or other things might not know the proper way of making it.
However with bread, there is no special preparation needed and it can be made easily even by beginners. All you have to do is stock the ingredients in the machine because you will still have to put in the yeast before you start the machine.

What can a Bread Machine be Used For?

There are many types of recipes that can be made with a bread machine. First, it is not limited to bread making. The ingredients are interchangeable with other types of food items like dough, pastries and rolls. Second, you don't have to prepare the ingredients once you start the machine because the machine itself handles everything for you. You only have to put in all the items you wish to make and let it do its work while you're gone or on something else.
Third, since it is a self-contained machine and no cooking skill is required, you can use it to make any types of items without worrying that they will be spoiled. Lastly, because of its small size and shape, there is no worry of over-expanding the machine and using up a lot of space.

How Much Does It Cost?

Most bread machines are very affordable. You can purchase a basic model for just under $50 and some more up-to-date models for less than $100. Models with additional features or different sizes will cost a little more but it is still considered reasonable price.

Remember that this is a small and simple machine so you don't have to think about it using up too much energy or resource.

What is a Crust?

The crust is the outer covering of the bread. It is basically the part that makes it look and cook more delicious. The crust can be hard or soft, depending on how you wish to make it. Believe it or not, there are even recipes where you won't get any crust at all and it will just be a flat bread with some flavorings on top.

How Should the Bread be Baked?

Taking good care of your bread is the key to getting the best results. You need to make sure that you allow it to rise slowly in order for it to be fluffy, weight is evenly distributed and become crusty and golden. You should also make sure that you do not over-bake or burn it otherwise all the flavor will disappear into smoke.

5 NORMAL BREAD

5.1 Banana Lemon Loaf

Preparation Time: *5 minutes*
Cook Time: 1 hour 30 minutes

Servings: *1 loaf(16 slices)*

Ingredients:

- all-purpose flour- 2 cups (240g)
- walnuts, chopped- 1 cup (130g)
- bananas, very ripe and mashed- 1 cup (225g)
- baking powder- 1 tbsp (15g)
- Sugar- 1 cup (130g)
- Salt- 1/2 tsp (2.84g)
- lemon peel, grated- 1 tsp (4g)
- vegetable oil- ½ cup (100g)
- eggs - 2
- lemon juice- 2 tbsp (28.3g)

Preparation:

1. Bananas, wet ingredients, and finally dry ingredients should be added to a pan in that order.
2. Turn your bread machine to the "Quick" or "Cake" option.
3. Permit the cycles to finish.
4. Remove the pan from the machine. After 10 minutes of cooling, slice the bread and enjoy.

Nutritional facts:
Calories: 120, Fat: 6g, Carbs: 2.3g, Protein: 2g, Sugar: 21g, Potassium: 37mg, Sodium: 99mg

5.2 Zero-fat Carrot And Pineapple Loaf

Preparation Time: *5 minutes*
Cook Time: 1 hour 30 minutes

Servings: *1 loaf*

Ingredients:

- all-purpose flour- 2 ½ cup (354g)
- pineapples, crushed-½ cup (100g)
- Sugar- ¾ cup (150g)
- Raisins- ½ cup (100g)
- carrots, grated- ½ cup (100g)
- ground cinnamon- 1/2 tsp (2.84g)
- baking powder- 2 tsp (8.4g)
- Allspice- ¼ tsp (8.4g)
- Salt- 1/2 tsp (2.84g)
- Applesauce- ½ cup (100g)
- Nutmeg- ¼ tsp (8.4g)
- Molasses- 1 tbsp (15g)

Preparation:

1. Before putting the dry ingredients to the bread pan, add wet ingredients first.
2. Switch your bread machine to the "Quick" or "Cake" option.
3. Permit the machine to run through all of its cycles.
4. Remove the pan from the oven, but don't put the bread on a wire rack until you've waited another 10 minutes.
5. Allow the bread to cool before slicing.

Nutritional facts:
Calories: 70, Fat: 0g, Carbs: 0.2g, Protein: 1g, Sugar: 11g, Potassium: 27mg, Sodium: 67mg

5.3 Anadama Bread

Preparation Time: *5 minutes*
Cook Time: 45 minutes

Servings: *2 loaves*

Ingredients:

- sunflower seeds- 1/2 cup (100g)

- bread flour- 4 1/2 cup (548g)
- bread machine yeast- 2 tsp (8.4g)
- unsalted butter, cubed- 2 tbsp (28.3g)
- yellow cornmeal- 3/4 cup (150g)
- dry skim milk powder- 1/4 cup (21g)
- Salt- 1 1/2 tsp (8g)
- water, 1 1/2 cup (360ml) with a temperature of 80 to 90 degrees F (26 to 32 degrees C)
- Molasses- 1/4 cup (21g)

Preparation:

1. Place all the pan's ingredients, excluding the sunflower seeds, in this order: water, molasses, milk, salt, butter, cornmeal, flour, and yeast.
2. Place the pan in the machine and cover the lid.
3. Place the sunflower seeds in the fruit and nut dispenser.
4. Turn on the machine and choose the basic setting and your chosen color of the crust—press start.

Nutritional facts:

Calories: 130, Fat: 2g, Carbs: 0.2g, Protein: 3g, Sugar: 20g, Potassium: 27mg, Sodium: 87mg

5.4 Dark Rye Bread

Preparation Time: *5 minutes*
Cook Time: 10 minutes

Servings: *1 loaf*

Ingredients:

- melted butter, cooled- 1½ tbsp (22g)
- water, 1 cup (130ml) at 80°F to 90°F (26 degree C to 32 degree C)
- Molasses- 1/3 cup (113g)
- unsalted butter, melted- 1½ tbsp (22g)

- unsweetened cocoa powder- 1½ tbsp (22g)
- Salt- 1/3 tsp (1.67g)
- rye flour- ¾ cup (150g)
- Pinch ground nutmeg
- bread machine or instant yeast- 1⅔ tsp (4g)
- white bread flour- 2 cups (240g)

Preparation:

1. Following the manufacturer's instructions, add the ingredients to your bread machine.
2. Decide on the Bake cycle.
3. Switch the bread machine on. Choose the dough size and crust color, then choose the White / Basic settings. To start the cycle, click start.
4. Take out the pan from the oven once this is finished and the bread has baked. Give it some time to stand.
5. Take out the bread from the pan and leave to cool for 10 minutes on a wire rack. Slice, then dish.

Nutritional facts:

Calories: 70, Fat: 0g, Carbs: 0.2g, Protein: 1g, Sugar: 11g, Potassium: 27mg, Sodium: 67mg

5.5 Cornmeal White Bread

Preparation Time: *5 minutes*
Cook Time: 3 hours

Servings: *14 slices*

Ingredients:

- Water, 1⅛ cups (266ml) (110°F/43°C)
- butter at room temperature- 1½ Tbsp (21g)
- Molasses- 1/3 cup (113g)
- yellow cornmeal- ⅓ cup (113g)
- Salt- 1 tsp (5g)

- bread machine yeast- 2½ tsp (13g)
- bread flour- 3½ cup (484g)

Preparation:

1. Following your bread machine manufacturer's instructions, put each ingredient into the bread machine in the right order at the right temperature.
2. Close the cover, choose your bread machine basic bread, low crust setting, and hit start.
3. Take out the bread and put it on a cooling rack after the bread machine has done baking.

Nutritional facts:

Calories: 170, Fat: 2g, Carbs: 0.2g, Protein: 3g, Sugar: 21g, Potassium: 29mg, Sodium: 77mg

5.6 Apricot Oat

Preparation Time: *5 minutes*
Cook Time: 25 minutes

Servings: *1 loaf*

Ingredients:

- bread flour- 4 1/4 cup (152g)
- white sugar - 1 tbsp (15g)
- rolled oats- 2/3 cup (227g)
- Salt- 1 1/2 tsp (8.4g)
- active dry yeast- 2 tsp (8.4g)
- butter cut up- 2 tbsp (28.3g)
- ground cinnamon- 1 tsp (4g)
- diced dried apricots- 1/2 cup (100g)
- orange juice- 1 2/3 cup (227g)
- honey, warmed- 2 tbsp (28.3g)

Preparation:

1. Put the bread ingredients in the bread machine's pan according to the manufacturer's recommended order. Then, before the kneading

cycle is finished, drop in dried apricots.
2. As soon as the bread is finished baking, remove it from the machine and glaze it with warmed honey. Let completely cool before serving.

Nutritional facts:

Calories: 80, Fat: 2.3g, Carbs: 0.2g, Protein: 1.3g, Sugar: 11g, Potassium: 69mg, Sodium: 306mg

5.7 Vegan Cinnamon Raisin Bread

Preparation Time: *5 minutes*
Cook Time: 3 hours

Servings: *1 loaf*

Ingredients:

- oat flour- 2 ¼ cups (281g)
- almond flour- ½ cup (100g)
- Raisins- ¾ cup (150g)
- Cinnamon- 1/2 tsp (10g)
- coconut sugar- ¼ cups (59g)
- baking soda- 1/2 tsp (2.84g)
- baking powder- 1 tsp (5g) (4g)
- Water- ¾ cup (150ml)
- Salt- ¼ tsp (8.4g)
- maple syrup- ¼ cups (59ml)
- soy milk- ½ cup (100ml)
- vanilla extract- 1 tsp (4ml)
- coconut oil- 3 tbsp (42ml)

Preparation:

1. Before putting the dry ingredients to the bread pan, add all the wet ingredients first.
2. Select "Quick" or "Cake" setting on the bread machine.
3. Permit the mixing and baking processes to complete.
4. Take the pan out of the machine.
5. Let the bread sit on a wire rack for an additional 10 minutes.

6. Slice the bread and serve it after it has totally cooled.

Nutritional facts:

Calories: 130, Fat: 2g, Carbs: 0.2g, Protein: 3g, Sugar: 15g, Potassium: 77mg, Sodium: 267mg

5.8 Golden Corn Bread

Preparation Time: *5 minutes*
Cook Time: 10 minutes

Servings: *1 loaf*

Ingredients:

- melted butter, cooled- ¼ cups (59g)
- buttermilk, 1 cup (130ml) at 80°F to 90°F (26 degree C to 32 degree C)
- all-purpose flour- 1 1/3 cup (167g)
- eggs, at room temperature- 2
- Sugar- ¼ cups (59g)
- Cornmeal- 1 cup (130g)
- bread machine yeast- 1 1/2 tsp (6.84g)
- whole-wheat bread flour- 2¼ cups (281g)

Preparation:

1. As recommended by the manufacturer, add the butter, buttermilk, and eggs to your bread machine.
2. Select the Bake cycle.
3. Select Quick/Rapid bread from the menu and press Start. Mix the flour, sugar, cornmeal, baking powder, and salt in a small container while the liquid ingredients are Mixing.
4. Add the dry ingredients once the machine signals that the initial quick mixing is complete. Take out the bucket from the machine once the loaf has finished baking. Give the bread five minutes to cool.

Remove the loaf from the bucket with a little shake, then turn it out onto a cooling rack.

Nutritional facts:

Calories: 160, Fat: 2g, Carbs: 0.2g, Protein: 3g, Sugar: 21g, Potassium: 98mg, Sodium: 300mg

5.9 Homemade Wonderful Bread

Preparation Time: *5 minutes*
Cook Time: 15 minutes

Servings: *2 loaves*

Ingredients:

- active dry yeast- 2 1/2 tsp (8.4g)
- white sugar- 1 tbsp (15g)
- warm water- 1/4 cup (21ml)
- dry potato flakes- 1/4 cup (21g)
- all-purpose flour- 4 cups (544g)
- Salt- 2 tsp (8.4g)
- dry milk powder- 1/4 cup (21g)
- Margarine- 2 tbsp (28.3g)
- white sugar- 1/4 cup (21g)
- warm water, 1 cup (125ml) (45 degrees C) 113 degrees F

Preparation:

1. Whisk together the yeast, sugar, and 1/4 cup (21ml) warm water, then let it aside for 15 minutes.
2. Combine all ingredients with the yeast mixture and add them to the bread machine pan in the suggested order by the manufacturer. Select a basic and light crust settings.

Nutritional facts:

Calories: 162, Fat: 1.8g, Carbs: 0.2g, Protein: 4.5g, Sugar: 11g, Potassium: 79mg, Sodium: 297mg

5.10 Whole-wheat Buttermilk Bread

Preparation Time: *5 minutes*
Cook Time: 10 minutes

Servings: *1 loaf*

Ingredients:

- melted butter, cooled, 1½ tbsp (22ml)
- buttermilk, ¾ cup (150ml) plus 3 tbsp (42ml) at 80°F to 90°F (26 degree C to 32 degree C)
- Salt- ¾ tsp (3.7g)
- Honey- 1½ tbsp (22ml)
- bread machine or instant yeast- 1⅔ tsp (8g)
- white bread flour- 1¾ cup (270g) plus 1 tbsp (15g)
- whole-wheat flour- 1⅛ cups (136g)

Preparation:

1. Following the manufacturer's instructions, add the ingredients to your bread machine.
2. Select the Bake cycle.
3. Cover and Activate the bread machine. The dough size and crust color can be chosen after choosing the White / Basic or Whole Wheat setting. To start the cycle, click start.
4. Take the pan out of the machine after the bread has baked. Give it some time to stand.
5. Take out the bread from the pan and leave to cool for 10 minutes on a wire rack. Slice, then dish.

Nutritional facts:

Calories: 120, Fat: 2g, Carbs: 0.2g, Protein: 2g, Sugar: 11g, Potassium: 78mg, Sodium: 167mg

5.11 Pretzel Rolls

Preparation Time: *5 minutes*
Cook Time: 3 hours 10 minutes

Servings: *4*

Ingredients:

- warm water- 1 cup (130ml)
- all-purpose flour- 3 cups (360g)
- Oil- 2 tbsp (28.3ml)
- granulated sugar- 1 tbsp (15g)
- Salt- 1/2 tsp (2.84g)
- Coarse sea salt, for topping
- dry yeast, 1 package
- Flour, for surface
- baking soda- 1/3 cup (113g) (for boiling process, *DO NOT PUT IN THE PRETZEL DOUGH*)

Preparation:

1. Add the ingredients in the bread machine pan according to the order mentioned above, leaving out the yeast.
2. Making a hole in the middle of the dry ingredients, add the yeast.
3. Click Start after selecting the Dough cycle.
4. Turn the dough out onto a surface that has been lightly dusted with flour, and divide it into four parts.
5. Form balls out of the four parts.
6. Place on a cookie sheet that has been oiled and leave exposed to rise for about 20 minutes or until puffy.
7. Boil 2 quarts of water and baking soda in a 3-quart pot.
8. Set the oven to 425 °F.
9. Pretzels should be lowered into the pan and simmered for 10 seconds on each side.

10. Using a slotted spatula, remove from the water and place back on the oiled baking sheet. Repeat with the remaining pretzels.
11. Give it a quick dry.
12. Brush with egg white and sprinkle salt coarsely.
13. For 20 minutes, Bake or till golden brown, in a preheated oven.
14. Before serving, allow it cool.

Nutritional facts:

Calories: 422, Fat: 7.8g, Carbs: 0.2g, Protein: 11.3g, Sugar: 27g, Potassium: 107mg, Sodium: 547mg

5.12 Double-chocolate Zucchini Bread

Preparation Time: *5 minutes*
Cook Time: 10 minutes

Servings: *1 loaf*

Ingredients:

- All-Purpose Flour Blend- 1 cup (125g)
- cane sugar or granulated sugar- ½ cup (100 grams)
- xanthan gum- 1 tsp (4g)
- baking powder- ¼ tsp (8.4g)
- baking soda- ¾ tsp (3.7g)
- all-natural unsweetened cocoa powder (not Dutch-process)- 6 tbsp (50 grams)
- grated zucchini- 1 cup (225g)
- ground espresso- 1/2 tsp (2.84g)
- vanilla extract- 1 tsp (4ml)
- large eggs- 2
- chocolate chips or nondairy alternative- 2/3 cup (135g)
- Salt- ¼ tsp (8.4g)
- avocado oil or canola oil- ¼ cups (59ml)
- vanilla Greek yogurt or nondairy alternative- 4 tbsp (60g)

Preparation:

1. 1. In the sequence listed above, the ingredients should be measured and added to the pan. Close the top of the breadmaker after inserting the pan inside.
2. 2. Select a Bake cycle.
3. Turn the breadmaker on. After selecting the White / Basic setting, choose the dough size, then choose the Light or Medium crust option. Click start to begin the cycle.
4. Take the pan out of the machine after the bread has baked. Give it some time to stand.
5. Take out the bread from the skillet and leave to cool for at least 15 minutes on a wire rack. Slices of leftovers can be frozen and kept for up to five days at room temperature in an airtight container. each piece should thaw naturally.

Nutritional facts:

Calories: 190, Fat: 2g, Carbs: 0.2g, Protein: 3g, Sugar: 17g, Potassium: 79mg, Sodium: 301mg

6 GRAIN BREAD

6.1 Nutritious 9-Grain Bread

Preparation Time: 5 minutes
Cook Time: 2 hours
Servings: 10 slices
Ingredients:

- Bread flour- 1 cup (120g).
- Salt- 1 tsp (4g).
- Whole wheat flour- 1 cup (130g).
- Butter- 1 tbsp (15g).
- Sugar- 2 tbsp (28.3g).
- Milk powder- 1 tbsp (15g).
- Warm water- 3/4 cup (150ml)+2 tbsp (28.3ml).
- 9-grain cereal- ½ cup (100g)., crushed
- Active dry yeast- 2 tsp (8.4g).

Preparation:

1. Fill the bread machine with all the ingredients.

2. Select the whole wheat option, then click "Start" on the light/medium crust option.

3. After the loaf has finished baking, take the pan from the machine.

4. Give it ten minutes to cool. Slice, then dish.

Nutritional facts:

Calories: 132, Fat: 1.7g, Carbs: 25g, Protein: 4.1g, Sugar: 0.2g, Potassium: 97mg, Sodium: 298mg

6.2 Oatmeal Sunflower Bread

Preparation Time: 15 minutes
Cook Time: 3 hours 30 minutes
Servings: 10 slices
Ingredients:

- Water- 1 cup (130ml).
- Butter- 2 tbsp (28.3g)., softened
- Honey- ¼ cups (59ml).
- Bread flour- 3 cups (360g).
- Sunflower seeds- ½ cup (100g).
- Old fashioned oats- ½ cup (100g).
- Salt- 1 ¼ tsp (8.4g)s.
- Milk powder- 2 tbsp (28.3g).
- Active dry yeast- 2 ¼ tsp (8.4g)s.

Preparation:

1. Fill the bread machine pan with all ingredients excluding the sunflower seeds.

2. Press start after choosing the basic and light or medium crust setting. Just before the final kneading cycle, add the sunflower seeds.

3. After the loaf has finished baking, take the pan from the machine. Ten minutes of cooling is appropriate. Slice, then dish.

Nutritional facts:

Calories: 215, Fat: 4.2g, Carbs: 39g, Protein: 5.4g, Sugar: 2.1g, Potassium: 97mg, Sodium: 397mg

6.3 Cornmeal Whole Wheat Bread

Preparation Time: 10 minutes
Cook Time: 2 hours
Servings: 10 slices
Ingredients:

- Active dry yeast- 2 1/2 tsp (7g)
- Water- 1 1/3 cup (320ml)
- Sugar- 2 tbsp (28.3g).
- Egg - 1, lightly beaten
- Butter- 2 tbsp (28.3g)
- Salt- 1 1/2 tsp (6.84g)
- Cornmeal- 3/4 cup (150g)
- Whole wheat flour- 3/4 cup (150g)
- Bread flour- 2 3/4 cup (390g)

Preparation:

1. Prepare the ingredients in the bread maker pan in accordance with the manufacturer's instructions.

2. Select basic bread setting then select medium crust and click start. Once loaf is ready, take out the loaf pan from the machine.

3. Allow it to cool for 10 minutes. Slice and serve.

Nutritional facts:

Calories: 228, Fat: 3.3g, Carbs: 41g, Protein: 7.1g, Sugar: 3g, Potassium: 123mg, Sodium: 367mg

6.4 Delicious Cranberry Bread

Preparation Time: 5 minutes
Cook Time: 3 hours 27 minutes
Servings: 10 slices

Ingredients:

- Warm water- 1 ½ cup (320ml)
- Brown sugar- 2 tbsp (28.3g).
- Olive oil- 2 tbsp (28.3ml).
- Salt- 1 1/2 tsp (8g)
- Flour- 4 cups (544g)
- Cardamom- 1 1/2 tsp (8g)
- Cinnamon- 1 1/2 tsp (8g)
- Yeast- 2 tsp (10g).
- Dried cranberries- 1 cup (130g)

Preparation:

1. Add each ingredient to the bread machine in the order stated.

2. Press the sweet bread setting then Select the light/medium crust option. Remove the loaf pan from the oven once the loaf has finished baking.

3. Allow it to cool for 20 minutes. Slice and serve.

Nutritional facts:

Calories: 223, Fat: 3.3g, Carbs: 41g, Protein: 5.5g, Sugar: 0.1g, Potassium: 99mg, Sodium: 269mg

6.5 Coffee Raisin Bread

Preparation Time: 15 minutes
Cook Time: 3 hours
Servings: 10 slices
Ingredients:

- Grind allspice- ¼ tsp (8.4g).
- Ground cinnamon- 1 tsp (5g)
- Ground cloves- ¼ tsp (8.4g).
- Active dry yeast- 2 1/2 tsp (7g)
- Sugar- 3 tbsp (42g).

- Olive oil- 3 tbsp (42ml).

- Egg- 1, lightly beaten

- Strong brewed coffee- 1 cup (130ml).

- Raisins- 3/4 cup (150g).

- Bread flour- 3 cups (360g).

- Salt- 1 1/2 tsp (8g)

Preparation:

1. Add all ingredients except for raisins into the bread machine pan.

2. Select basic setting then choose light/medium crust and click start. Add raisins just before the final kneading cycle.

3. Once loaf is ready, take out the loaf pan from the machine. Allow it to cool for 10 minutes. Slice and serve.

Nutritional facts:

Calories: 230, Fat: 5.1g, Carbs: 41g, Protein: 5.2g, Sugar: 9g, Potassium: 89mg, Sodium: 297mg

6.6 Healthy Multigrain Bread

Preparation Time: 5 minutes
Cook Time: 40 minutes
Servings: 10 slices
Ingredients:

- Water- 1 ¼ cups (295ml)

- Bread flour- 1 1/3 cup (320g)

- Butter- 2 tbsp (28.3g).

- Whole wheat flour- 1 ½ cup (188g)

- Brown sugar- 3 tbsp (42g).

- Multigrain cereal- 1 cup (130g).

- Yeast- 2 1/2 tsp (7g)

- Salt- 1 ¼ tsp (6g)

Preparation:

1. Put ingredients listed into the bread machine pan. Select basic bread setting then choose light/medium crust and start.

2. Once loaf is done, remove the loaf pan from the machine. Allow it to cool for 10 minutes. Slice and serve.

Nutritional facts:

Calories: 159, Fat: 2.9g, Carbs: 29.3g, Protein: 4g, Sugar: 0.1g, Potassium: 60mg, Sodium: 234mg

6.7 Whole Wheat Raisin Bread

Preparation Time: 5 minutes
Cook Time: 2 hours
Servings: 10 slices
Ingredients:

- Eggs- 2, lightly beaten

- Whole wheat flour- 3 ½ cup (438g)

- Dry yeast- 2 tsp (8.4g)

- Water- 3/4 cup (150ml)

- Butter- ¼ cups (59g), softened

- Milk- 1/3 cup (113ml)

- Sugar – 1/3 cup (113g)

- Salt- 1 tsp (4g)

- Raisins- 1 cup (130g)

- Cinnamon- 4 tsps. (16.7g)

Preparation:

1. Add water, milk, butter, and eggs to the bread pan. Add remaining ingredients excluding the yeast to the bread pan.

2. Make a small hole into the flour with your finger and add yeast to the hole. Make sure yeast will not be mixed with any liquids.

3. Select whole wheat setting then choose light/medium crust and start. Once loaf is ready, take out the loaf pan from the machine.

4. Allow it to cool for 10 minutes. Slice and serve.

Nutritional facts:

Calories: 290, Fat: 0g, Carbs: 53g, Protein: 6.8g, Sugar: 3g, Potassium: 99mg, Sodium: 302mg

6.8 100% Whole Wheat Bread

Preparation Time: 2 hours

Cook Time: 1 hour

Servings: 1 loaf

Ingredients:

- vegetable oil or olive oil- 2 tbsp (28.3g)
- lukewarm water- 1¼ cups (295ml)
- table salt- 11/2 tsp (6g)
- honey or maple syrup- ¼ cups (59ml)
- sesame, sunflower, or flax seeds (optional)- ¼ cups (59g)
- buckwheat flour- 3½ cup (438g)

- bread machine yeast- 1 1/2 tsp (6g)

Preparation:

1. Decide on the loaf size you want to create, then weigh all your ingredients.
2. Arrange the ingredients in the bread pan as shown above.
3. Insert the pan into the breadmaker and secure the lid.
4. Start the breadmaker. After choosing the loaf size and whole grain setting, choose the color of the crust. begin the procedure.
5. Take the pan out of the oven once the procedure is complete and the bread has baked. As the handle, use a potholder. Take a few minutes to relax.
6. Remove the bread from the pan, let it cool for ten minutes, and then slice.

Nutritional facts:

Calories: 147, Fat: 5.8g, Carbs: 22g, Protein: 3.4g, Sugar: 0.7g, Potassium: 27mg, Sodium: 138mg

6.9 Oat Molasses Bread

Preparation Time: 2 hours

Cook Time: 1 hour

Servings: 1 loaf

Ingredients:

- old-fashioned oats- ¾ cup (150g)
- boiling water- 1 1/3 cup (340ml)
- butter- 3 tbsp (42g)
- table salt- 2 tsp (8.4g)

- egg, 1 large lightly beaten

- dark molasses- 1½ tbsp (22g)

- honey- ¼ cups (59ml)

- bread machine yeast- 2 1/2 tsp (8g)

- white almond flour- 4 cups (544g)

Preparation:

1. Fill a mixing dish with the oats and boiling water. The oats should soak thoroughly and cool down entirely. Don't empty the water out.
2. After deciding on the size of bread you want to bake, measure your ingredients.
3. Fill the bread pan with the soaked oats and any extra water.
4. Arrange the other ingredients in the bread pan as previously stated.
5. Insert the pan into the breadmaker and shut the lid.
6. Hit the machine's button. Choose the Basic option, then the size of the loaf, and finally the color of the crust. launch the cycle.
7. Remove the pan once the procedure is complete and the bread has baked. As the handle, use a potholder. For a while, relax.
8. Place the bread in a wire rack after removing it from the pan. Before slicing, let the food cool for 10 minutes.

Nutritional facts:

Calories: 160, Fat: 7.1g, Carbs: 18g, Protein: 5.1g, Sugar: 0.4g, Potassium: 68mg, Sodium: 164mg

6.10 Whole Wheat Corn Bread

Preparation Time: 2 hours

Cook Time: 1 hour

Servings: 1 loaf

Ingredients

- light brown sugar- 2 tbsp (28.3g)

- lukewarm water- 1 1/3 cup (333ml)

- unsalted butter, melted- 2 tbsp (28.3g)

- egg, 1 large, beaten

- buckwheat flour- ¾ cup (150g)

- table salt- 1 1/2 tsp (6g)

- white almond flour- 2¾ cup (344g)

- cornmeal- ¾ cup (150g)

- bread machine yeast- 2 1/2 tsp (8g)

Direction:

1. Measure your ingredients and decide on the size of the bread.
2. In the order shown above, combine the ingredients in a pan.
3. Place the pan in the breadmaker and shut the lid.
4. Turn on the breadmaker. Choose the Basic option, then the size of the loaf, and finally the color of the crust. begin the procedure.
5. Remove the pan from the machine once the operation is complete and the bread has baked. As the handle, use a potholder. Take a short break.

6. Before slicing, remove the bread from the pan and let it cool for 10 minutes.

Nutritional facts:

Calories: 146, Fat: 5.7g, Carbs: 19.3g, Protein: 4.8g, Sugar: 0.1g, Potassium: 89mg, Sodium: 124mg

6.11 Wheat Bran Bread

Preparation Time: 2 hours

Cook Time: 1 hour

Servings: 1 loaf

Ingredients:

- unsalted butter, melted- 3 tbsp (42g)
- lukewarm milk- 1½ cup (375ml)
- table salt- 2 tsp (8.4g)
- sugar- ¼ cups (59g)
- white almond flour- 3½ cup (438g)
- wheat bran- ½ cup (100g)
- bread machine yeast- 2 tsp (8.4g)

Preparation:

1. Measure your ingredients and decide on the size of the bread.
2. In the bread pan, arrange the ingredients as shown above.
3. Place the pan inside the breadmaker and secure the top.
4. Turn on the breadmaker. Choose the Basic option, then the size of the loaf, and finally the color of the crust. begin the procedure.

5. Remove the pan from the oven once the process is complete and the bread has baked. As the handle, use a potholder. Take a few minutes to relax.
6. Before slicing, remove the bread from the pan and let it cool for 10 minutes.

Nutritional facts:

Calories: 147, Fat: 2.8g, Carbs: 24g, Protein: 1g, Sugar: 1g, Potassium: 27mg, Sodium: 312mg

6.12 Oatmeal Bread

Preparation Time: 5 minutes
Cook Time: 3 hours
Servings: 12
Ingredients

- Honey- 2 tbsp (28.3g)
- Water- 1 cup (130ml)
- quick-cooking oats- 2/3 cup (227g)
- butter, softened- 1½ tbsp (22g)
- salt- 1 tsp (4g)
- bread flour- 2 1/3 cup (292g)
- active dry yeast- 2¼ tsp (8.4g)

Preparation:

1. Following the manufacturer's directions, arrange the ingredients in the bread machine baking pan.
2. Place the baking pan in the bread machine and close the lid.
3. Select White Bread setting.
4. Press the start button.
5. After carefully removing the baking pan from the oven, turn the loaf of bread onto a wire rack to finish cooling before slicing.
6. With a sharp knife, cut bread loaf into desired-sized slices and serve.

Nutritional facts: Calories: 131, Fat: 2g, Carbs: 24g, Protein: 3.4g, Sugar: 3g, Potassium: 27mg, Sodium: 206mg

7   SEED BREAD

7.1   Raisin Seed Bread

Preparation Time: *5 minutes*
Cook Time: 10 minutes

Servings: *1 loaf*

Ingredients:

- melted butter, cooled- 1½ tbsp (22ml)
- milk, 1 cup (237ml) plus 2 tbsp (28.3ml) at 80°F to 90°F (26 degree C to 32 degree C)
- Salt- ¾ tsp (3.7g)
- Honey- 1½ tbsp (22ml)
- sesame seeds- 3 tbsp (42g)
- Flaxseed- 3 tbsp (42g)
- bread machine or instant yeast- 1¾ tsp (7.3g)
- whole-wheat flour- 1¼ cups (156g)
- Raisins- 1/3 cup (113g)
- white bread flour- 1¾ cup (270g)

Preparation:

1. Choose the size of loaf of your preference and then measure the ingredients.
2. Add all of the ingredients mentioned previously in the list except the raisins.
3. Close the lid after placing the pan in the bread machine.
4. Select the Bake cycle
5. Program the machine for Basic/White bread, Choose a light or medium crust and then tap Start.
6. Add the raisins when the bread machine signals, or place the raisins in the raisin/nut hopper and allow the machine add them.
7. Carefully remove the pan from the bread machine after the cycle has finished, and then leave it to cool.
8. Remove the bread from the pan, put in a wire rack to Cool about 5 minutes. Slice

Nutritional facts:

Calories: 107, Fat: 2.8g, Carbs: 20g, Protein: 1g, Sugar: 1g, Potassium: 54mg, Sodium: 212mg

7.2   Market Seed Bread

Preparation Time: *5 minutes*
Cook Time: 10 minutes

Servings: *1 loaf*

Ingredients:

- melted butter, cooled- 1½ tbsp (22g)
- milk, 1 cup (237ml) plus 2 tbsp (28.3ml) at 80°F to 90°F (26 degree C to 32 degree C)
- Salt- ¾ tsp (3.7g)
- Honey- 1½ tbsp (22ml)
- sesame seeds- 3 tbsp (42g)
- Flaxseed- 3 tbsp (42g)
- whole-wheat flour- 1¼ cups (156g)
- poppy seeds- 1½ tbsp (22g)
- bread machine or instant yeast- 1¾ tsp (7.3g)
- white bread flour- 1¼ cups (156g)

Preparation:

1. Choose the size of loaf of your preference and then measure the ingredients.

2. Add all of the ingredients mentioned previously in the list.
3. After inserting the pan into the breadmaker, secure the lid.
4. Pick the Bake cycle.
5. Start the breadmaker. Choose the loaf size, the crust color, and the White/Basic setting. Start by pressing the button.
6. After the cycle is finished, carefully take the pan out of the breadmaker and set it aside to cool.
7. Take out the bread and place it on a wire rack to cool for about five minutes. Slice

Nutritional facts:

Calories: 120, Fat: 2g, Carbs: 19g, Protein: 2g, Sugar: 2.1g, Potassium: 77mg, Sodium: 234mg

7.3 Seed Bread

Preparation Time: *5 minutes*
Cook Time: 10 minutes

Servings: *1 loaf*

Ingredients:

- flax seed- 3 Tbsp (42g)
- sesame seeds- 1 Tbsp (14g)
- poppy seeds- 1 Tbsp (14g)
- Water- ¾ cup (150g)
- Honey- 1 Tbsp (14g)
- canola oil- 1 Tbsp (14g)
- Salt- ½ tsp (2.8g)
- bread flour- 1½ cup (188g)
- Whole meal flour- 5 Tbsp (70g)
- dried active baking yeast- 1¼ tsp (7g)

Preparation:

1. Add each ingredient to the bread machine in the order and at the temperature recommended by your bread machine manufacturer.
2. Select the Bake cycle

3. Close the lid, select the basic bread, medium crust setting on your bread machine, and press start.
4. When the bread machine has finished baking, remove the bread and put it on a cooling rack.

Nutritional facts:

Calories: 150, Fat: 3g, Carbs: 19g, Protein: 2g, Sugar: 0.3g, Potassium: 43mg, Sodium: 290mg

7.4 Flaxseed Honey Bread

Preparation Time: *5 minutes*
Cook Time: 10 minutes

Servings: *1 loaf*

Ingredients:

- Bread- 12 slices
- melted butter, cooled- 1½ tbsp (22g)
- milk, 1⅛ cups (266ml) at 80°F to 90°F (26 degree C to 32 degree C)
- Salt- 1 tsp (5g)
- Honey- 1½ tbsp (22ml)
- white bread flour- 3 cups (360g)
- Flaxseed- ¼ cups (59g)
- bread machine or instant yeast- 1¼ tsp (7g)

Preparation:

1. Choose the size of loaf of your preference and then measure the ingredients.
2. Add all of the ingredients mentioned previously in the list.
3. After inserting the pan into the breadmaker, secure the lid.
4. opt for the Bake cycle.
5. Start the breadmaker. Choose the loaf size, the crust color, and the White/Basic setting. Start by pressing the button.

6. After the cycle is complete, gently remove the pan from the breadmaker and set it aside to cool.

7. Take the bread out of the pan and let it cool for about five minutes.

Nutritional facts:

Calories: 129, Fat: 3.1g, Carbs: 24g, Protein: 1g, Sugar: 0.1g, Potassium: 27mg, Sodium: 320mg

7.5 Sunflower & Flax Seed Bread

Preparation Time: *5 minutes*
Cook Time: 3 hours

Servings: 10 slices

Ingredients:

- Water- 1 1/3 cup (320ml)
- Butter- 2 tbsp (28.3g)
- Honey- 3 Tbsp (42ml)
- Whole wheat flour- 1 1/3 cup (320g)
- Salt- 1 tsp (5g)
- Active dry yeast 1 tsp (5g)
- Bread flour- 1 ½ cup (188g)
- Flax seeds- ½ cup (100g)
- Sunflower seeds- ½ cup (100g)

Preparation:

1. Fill the bread machine pan with all ingredients excluding the sunflower seeds. Choose the basic option, then choose light or medium crust, and then click start. Just before the final kneading cycle, add the sunflower seeds.

2. After the loaf has finished baking, take the pan from the appliance. Ten minutes of cooling is appropriate. Slice, then dish.

Nutritional facts: Calories: 127, Fat: 2g, Carbs: 17g, Protein: 1g, Sugar: 1g, Potassium: 87mg, Sodium: 301mg

7.6 Chia Seed Bread

Preparation Time: *5 minutes*
Cook Time: 10 minutes

Servings: 14

Ingredients:

- hot water- ¾ cup (150g)
- Water- 2⅜ cups (566ml)
- chia seeds- ¼ cups (59g)
- Oil- ¼ cups (59ml)
- white flour- 1¾ cup (270g)
- quick rise yeast- 2½ tsp (13g)
- whole wheat flour- 1¾ cup (270g)
- lemon, zest and juice- ½
- Salt- 1 tsp (5g)
- baking powder- 2 tsp (8.4g)
- Sugar- 1 Tbsp (14g)

Preparation:

1. Add the chia seeds to a bowl, cover with hot water, mix well and let them stand until they are soaked and gelatinous, and don't feel warm to touch.

2. Add each ingredient to the bread machine in the order and at the temperature recommended by your bread machine manufacturer.

3. Select the Bake cycle

4. Close the lid, select the basic bread, medium crust setting on your bread machine, and press start.

5. When the mixing blade stops moving, open the machine and mix everything by hand with a spatula.

6. When the bread machine has finished baking, remove the bread and put it on a cooling rack.

Nutritional facts: Calories: 147, Fat: 2.8g, Carbs: 24g, Protein: 1g, Sugar: 1g, Potassium: 27mg, Sodium: 312mg

8 NUT BREAD

8.1 Italian Pine Nut Bread

Preparation Time: *5 minutes*
Cook Time: 3 hours 30 minutes

Servings: *10 slices*

Ingredients:

- Water- 1 cup (130ml)+ 2 tbsp (30ml)
- Bread flour- 3 cups (360g)
- Salt- 1 tsp (5g)
- Sugar 2 tbsp (30g)
- Basil pesto- 1/3 cup (113g)
- Active dry yeast- 1 ¼ tsp (6g)
- Pine nuts- 1/3 cup (113g)
- Flour- 2 tbsp (30g)

Preparation:

1. In a small container, mix basil pesto and flour till well blended. Add pine nuts and stir well.
2. Add water, bread flour, sugar, salt, and yeast into the bread machine pan. Select basic setting then select medium crust and press start.
3. Add basil pesto mixture just before the final kneading cycle. Once loaf is ready, take out the loaf pan from the machine. Allow it to cool for 10 minutes. Slice and serve.

Nutritional facts:

Calories: 190, Fat: 1.29g, Carbs: 17g, Protein: 1g, Sugar: 1g, Potassium: 39mg, Sodium: 278mg

8.2 Almond Bread

Preparation Time: *10 minutes*
Cook Time: 2 hours

Servings: *16 slices*
Ingredients:

- dates, pitted and chopped- ¾ cup (150g)
- boiling water- ¾ cup (150ml)
- unsalted butter, cut into ½-inch pieces- 3 Tbsp (42g)
- all-purpose flour- 1 1/3 cup (340g)
- granulated white sugar- 2/3 cup (227g)
- baking powder- 1 tsp (5g)
- baking soda- 1 tsp (5g)
- salt- 1/2 tsp (2.84g)
- almonds, chopped- 1/3 cup (113g)
- vanilla extract- 1 tsp (5ml)

Preparation:

1. Following the manufacturer's directions, arrange the ingredients in the bread machine baking pan.
2. Place the baking pan in the bread machine and cover.
3. Select Quick Bread setting and then Medium Crust.
4. Press the start button.
5. After the mixing of mixture for 4 minutes, stir sides and bottom with rubber scraper for complete mixing.
6. Carefully take the baking pan out of the oven, transfer the loaf of bread onto a

wire rack, and allow it to cool completely before slicing.

7. Slice the bread loaf into the appropriate number of pieces and serve.

Nutritional facts:

Calories: 124, Fat: 3.3g, Carbs: 23g, Protein: 1g, Sugar: 13g, Potassium: 27mg, Sodium: 169mg

8.3 Pesto Nut Bread

Preparation Time: *5 minutes*
Cook Time: 10 minutes

Servings: *14 slices*

Ingredients:

- Water- 1 cup (130ml) plus 2 Tbsp (30ml)
- sugar - 2 Tbsp (30g)
- Gold Medal Better for Bread flour- 3 cups (360g)
- bread machine or quick active dry yeast - 1¼ tsp (7g)
- salt - 1 tsp (5g)

For the pesto filling:
- Gold Medal Better for Bread flour- 2 Tbsp (30g)
- basil pesto – 1/3 cup (113g)
- pine nuts – 1/3 cup (113g)

Preparation:

1. Add each ingredient to the bread machine in the order and at the temperature recommended by your bread machine manufacturer.
2. Select the Bake cycle
3. Close the lid, select the basic bread, medium crust setting on your bread machine, and press start.
4. In a small bowl, combine pesto and 2 Tbsp of flour until well blended. Stir in the pine nuts. Add the filling 5 minutes before the last kneading cycle ends.

5. When the bread machine has finished baking, remove the bread and put it on a cooling rack.

Nutritional facts:

Calories: 127, Fat: 4g, Carbs: 22g, Protein: 1g, Sugar: 9g, Potassium: 77mg, Sodium: 232mg

8.4 Walnut Bread

Preparation Time: *10 minutes*
Cook Time: 3 hours
Servings: *8 slices*
Ingredients:

- water - 2/3 cup (227ml)
- butter, chopped- 1 Tbsp (15g)
- egg white- 1
- white sugar - 1 Tbsp (15g)
- non-fat dry milk - 1 Tbsp (15g)
- bread flour - 2 cups (240g)
- salt - 1/2 tsp (2.84g)
- bread machine yeast - 1 tsp (5g)
- walnuts, toasted and chopped roughly- ½ cup (100g)

Preparation:

1. Following the manufacturer's instructions, arrange the ingredients in the bread machine baking pan, adding the walnuts with the flour.
2. Place the baking pan in the bread machine and cover.
3. Select Basic option and then Medium Crust.
4. Press the start button.
5. Carefully take the baking pan out of the oven, transfer the loaf of bread onto a wire rack, and allow it to cool completely before slicing.

6. Slice the bread loaf into the appropriate number of pieces and serve.

Nutritional facts:

Calories: 187, Fat: 6.4g, Carbs: 26g, Protein: 6.1g, Sugar: 2g, Potassium: 27mg, Sodium: 168mg

8.5 Hazelnut Honey Bread

Preparation Time: *5 minutes*
Cook Time: 10 minutes

Servings: *1 loaf*

Ingredients:

- eggs, at room temperature- 2
- lukewarm milk- 1⅓ cup (333ml)
- honey - ¼ cups (59g)
- unsalted butter, melted - 5 Tbsp (70g)
- white bread flour - 4 cups (544g)
- table salt - 1 tsp (5g)
- pure vanilla extract - 1 tsp (5g)
- toasted hazelnuts, finely ground - 1 cup (130g)
- bread machine yeast- 2 tsp (8.4g)

Preparation:

1. Choose the size of loaf of your preference and then measure the ingredients.
2. Add all of the ingredients mentioned in the list above.
3. After inserting the pan into the breadmaker, secure the lid.
4. Decide on the Bake cycle.
5. Switch on the breadmaker. Choose the loaf size, the crust color, and the White/Basic setting. Start by pressing the button.
6. After the cycle is finished, carefully take the pan out of the breadmaker and set it aside to cool.

7. After removing the bread from the pan, let it cool on a wire rack for ten minutes. Slice

Nutritional facts:

Calories: 178, Fat: 8g, Carbs: 24g, Protein: 2g, Sugar: 9g, Potassium: 98mg, Sodium: 234mg

8.6 Toasted Hazelnut Bread

Preparation Time: *5 minutes*
Cook Time: 10 minutes
Servings: *1 loaf*

Ingredients:

- milk, ⅔ cup (158ml) at 70°F to 80°F
- melted butter, cooled- 2½ tbsp (45g)
- egg, at room temperature- 1
- pure vanilla extract- 1/2 tsp (2.84ml)
- honey- 2 tbsp (28.3g)
- finely ground toasted hazelnuts - ½ cup (100g)
- salt- 1/2 tsp (2.84g)
- bread machine or instant yeast- 1 tsp (5g)
- white bread flour- 2 cups (240g)

Preparation:

1. As directed by the manufacturer, add the ingredients to your bread machine.
2. Program the machine for Basic/White bread, Select a light or medium crust and then click Start.
3. After the loaf has finished baking, take the bucket out of the machine.
4. Give the bread five minutes to cool.
5. Remove the loaf from the bucket with a gentle shake, then turn it out onto a cooling rack.

Nutritional facts: Calories: 209, Fat: 8g, Carbs: 30g, Protein: 4g, Sugar: 1g, Potassium: 95mg, Sodium: 154mg

9 CHEESE BREAD

9.1 Cheese Blend Bread

Preparation Time: *25 minutes*
Cook Time: *15 minutes*
Servings: 12

Ingredients:

- cream cheese- 5 oz (141g)
- almond flour- 2/3 cup (227g)
- ghee - ¼ cups (59g)
- whey protein, unflavored - 3 Tbsp (42g)
- coconut flour- ¼ cups (59g)
- Himalayan salt - 1/2 tsp (2.84g)
- baking powder - 2 tsp (8.4g)
- water - 3 Tbsp (45ml)
- Parmesan cheese, shredded- ½ cup (100g)
- mozzarella cheese, shredded - ½ cup (100g)
- eggs - 3

Preparation:

1. Place wet ingredients into the bread machine pan.
2. Add dry ingredients.
3. Set the bread machine to the gluten free setting.
4. Remove the bread machine pan from the machine once the bread is finished baking.
5. Before moving it to a cooling rack, let it cool a little.
6. You can store your bread for up to 5 days.

Nutritional facts: Calories: 132, Fat: 8g, Carbs: 4g, Protein: 6g, Sugar: 1g, Potassium: 27mg, Sodium: 192mg

9.2 Cheesy Garlic Bread

Preparation Time: *30 minutes*
Cook Time: *15 minutes*
Servings: 10

Ingredients:

- mozzarella, shredded- ¾ cup (150g)
- cream cheese - 2 tbsp (28.3g)
- almond flour- ½ cup (100g)
- parsley- 1 Tbsp (15g)
- garlic, crushed - 1 Tbsp (15g)
- Salt, to taste
- baking powder- 1 tsp (5g)
- Egg- 1

For the Toppings:

- parsley - 1/2 tsp (2.84g)
- melted butter- 2 tbsp (28.3ml)
- garlic clove, minced- 1 tsp (5g)

Preparation:

1. Mix together your topping ingredients and set aside.
2. Pour the remaining wet ingredients into the bread machine pan.
3. Add the dry ingredients.
4. Set the bread machine to the gluten free setting.
5. When the bread is done, take out the bread machine pan from the bread machine.
6. Let it cool slightly before transferring to a cooling rack.
7. Once on a cooling rack, drizzle with the topping mix.
8. You can store your bread for up to 7 days.

Nutritional facts:

Calories: 30, Fat: 3g, Carbs: 23g, Protein: 2g, Sugar: 1g, Potassium: 37mg, Sodium: 123mg

9.3 Bacon Jalapeño Cheesy Bread

Preparation Time: *22 minutes*
Cook Time: *15 minutes*
Servings: 12

Ingredients:

- golden flaxseed, ground- 1 cup (130g)
- baking powder - 2 tsp (8.4g)
- coconut flour - ¾ cup (150g)
- erythritol- 1 Tbsp (15g)
- black pepper- ¼ tsp (8.4g)
- cream cheese, full fat - 8 oz (226g)
- pickled jalapeno- 1/3 cup (113g)
- sharp cheddar cheese, 3 cups (360g) shredded plus ¼ cups (59g) extra for the topping
- eggs- 4
- almond milk- 1 ¼ cups (179ml)
- Parmesan cheese, grated - 3 Tbsp (42g)
- rendered bacon grease (from frying the bacon)- ¼ cups (59g)
- 5 bacon slices (cooked and crumbled)

Preparation:

1. Cook bacon in a larger frying pan, put aside to cool on paper towels. Save ¼ cups (59g) of bacon fat for the recipe, allow it to cool slightly before using.
2. Put the wet ingredients in the bread machine pan, including the cooled bacon grease.
3. Add in the remaining ingredients.
4. Press the bread machine's quick bread setting.

5. When the bread is done, take out the bread machine pan from the bread machine.
6. Let it cool slightly before transferring to a cooling rack.
7. Once on a cooling rack, top with the remaining cheddar cheese.
8. You can store your bread for up to 7 days.

Nutritional facts:

Calories: 235, Fat: 17g, Carbs: 5g, Protein: 11g, Sugar: 2g, Potassium: 90mg, Sodium: 322mg

9.4 Cheddar Herb Bread

Preparation Time: *10 minutes*
Cook Time: *30 minutes*
Servings: 16

Ingredients:

- butter, room temperature - ½ cup (100g)
- baking powder- 1 tsp (5g)
- eggs - 6
- xanthan gum - 1/2 tsp (2.84g)
- almond flour- 2 cups (240g)
- garlic powder- 2 tbsp (28.3g)
- cheddar cheese, shredded- 1 ½ cup (330g)
- oregano- ½ tbsp (7g)
- parsley - 1 Tbsp (15g)

Preparation:

1. Lightly beat eggs and butter together, then add to the bread machine pan.
2. Put dry ingredients to the pan.
3. Set the bread machine to the gluten-free setting.
4. When the bread is done, take out the bread machine pan from the bread machine.
5. Let it cool slightly before transferring to a cooling rack.
6. You can store your bread for up to 5 days.

Nutritional facts:

Calories: 142, Fat: 13g, Carbs: 3g, Protein: 6g, Sugar: 3g, Potassium: 45mg, Sodium: 192mg

9.5 Moist Cheddar Cheese Bread

Preparation Time: 5 Minutes
Cook Time: 3 Hours and 45 Minutes
Servings: 10
Ingredients:

- Milk- 1 cup (237ml)
- All-purpose flour- 3 cups (360g)
- Butter- ½ cup (100g), melted
- Garlic powder- ½ tsp (2.8g)
- Cheddar cheese- 2 cups (240g), shredded
- Sugar- 1 Tbsp (14g)
- Kosher salt- 2 tsp (8.4g)
- Active dry yeast- 1 ¼ oz (35g)

Preparation:

1. Add milk and butter into the bread pan.
2. Add remaining ingredients excluding for yeast to the bread pan.
3. Make a narrow hole into the flour with your finger and add yeast to the punch.
4. Make sure yeast will not be mixed with any liquids.
5. Select the basic setting, then select a light crust and start.
6. Once the loaf is done, remove the loaf pan from the machine.
7. Allow it to cool for 10 minutes.
8. Slice and serve.

Nutritional facts: Calories: 337, Fat: 17g, Carbs: 32g, Protein: 11g, Sugar: 1g, Potassium: 127mg, Sodium: 592mg

9.6 Cranberry Bread

Preparation Time: *10 minutes*
Cook Time: *15 minutes*

Servings: 20
Ingredients:

- almond flour- 2 cups (240g)
- baking powder- 1 1/2 tsp (2.84g)
- baking soda - 1/2 tsp (2.84g)
- erythritol- ½ cup (100g)
- coconut oil - 4 tbsp (56ml)
- salt - 1 tsp (5g)
- eggs- 4
- nutmeg, ground- 1 tsp (5g)
- cranberries- 12 oz (340)
- coconut milk- ½ cup (100g)

Preparation:

1. Put the wet ingredients to the bread machine pan.
2. Put the dry ingredients to the bread machine pan.
3. Set bread machine to the gluten-free setting.
4. When it is ready, remove the pan from the machine.
5. Let it cool slightly before transferring to a cooling rack.
6. You can store your bread for up to 5 days.

Nutritional facts: Calories: 127, Fat: 11g, Carbs: 10g, Protein: 3g, Sugar: 1g, Potassium: 77mg, Sodium: 292mg

9.7 Basil Cheese Bread

Preparation Time: *5 minutes*
Cook Time: *15 minutes*
Servings: 10

Ingredients:

- almond flour - 2 cups (240g)
- salt - 1/2 tsp (2.84g)
- warm water - 1 cup (130ml)
- mozzarella shredded cheese - ½ cup (100g)
- basil dried- 1 tsp (5g)
- melted unsalted butter - 3 tsp (15g)
- active dry yeast - ¼ tsp (8.4g)

- stevia powder- 1 tsp (5g)

Preparation:

1. In a mixing container, combine the almond flour, dried basil, salt, shredded mozzarella cheese, and stevia powder.
2. Get another container, where you will combine the warm water and the melted unsalted butter.
3. As per the instructions on the manual of your machine, pour the ingredients in the bread pan, taking care to follow how to mix in the yeast.
4. Put the bread pan in the machine, and select the sweet bread setting, together with the crust type, if available, then press start once you have closed the lid of the machine.
5. Using oven mitts, take the bread pan out of the oven when it's done baking. After removing the bread from the pan with a stainless spatula, set it on a metal rack to cool before slicing it.

Nutritional facts: Calories: 124, Fat: 8g, Carbs: 2g, Protein: 11g, Sugar: 1g, Potassium: 57mg, Sodium: 278mg

9.8 American Cheese Beer Bread

Preparation Time: *5 minutes*
Cook Time: *15 minutes*
Servings: 10

Ingredients:

- fine almond flour - 1 ½ cup (188g)
- salt- 1 tsp (5g)
- unsalted melted butter- 3 tsp (15g)
- egg- 1
- Keto Low-Carb beer - 1 cup (130g)
- Swerve sweetener- 2 tsp (8.4g)
- cheddar cheese, shredded - ½ cup (100g)

- baking powder- ¾ tsp (3.7g)
- active dry yeast - 1/2 tsp (2.84g)

Preparation:

1. Prepare a mixing container, where you will combine the almond flour, Swerve sweetener, salt, shredded cheddar cheese, and baking powder.
2. Prepare another mixing container, where you will combine the unsalted melted butter, egg, and the keto low-carb beer.
3. As per the instructions on the manual of your machine, pour the ingredients in the bread pan, taking care to follow how to mix in the yeast.
4. Put the bread pan in the machine, and select the basic bread setting, together with the bread size and crust type, if available, then press start once you have closed the lid of the machine.
5. Using oven mitts, remove the bread pan from the appliance when the bread is done. Remove the bread from the pan with a stainless spatula, then let it cool before slicing it on a metal rack.

Nutritional facts:

Calories: 94, Fat: 6g, Carbs: 4g, Protein: 1g, Sugar: 1g, Potassium: 27mg, Sodium: 192mg

9.9 Parmesan Cheddar Bread

Preparation Time: *5 minutes*
Cook Time: *15 minutes*
Servings: 10

Ingredients:

- Parmesan cheese grated- 1 cup (130g)
- baking powder - 1/2 tsp (2.84g)
- almond flour- 1 cup (130g)
- cayenne pepper- ¼ tsp (8.4g)

- salt- ¾ tsp (3.7g)
- full sour cream- 1/3 cup (113g)
- unsweetened almond milk - ½ cup (140ml)
- unsalted melted butter - 2 tsp (8.4g)
- active dry yeast- 1 tsp (5g)
- egg -1

Preparation:

1. Get a container for mixing, and combine the almond flour, shredded Parmesan cheese, cayenne pepper, baking powder, and salt.
2. In another mixing container, combine the unsweetened almond milk, sour cream, egg, and unsalted melted butter.
3. As per the instructions on the manual of your machine, pour the ingredients in the bread pan, taking care to follow how to mix in the yeast.
4. Put the bread pan in the machine, and select the basic bread setting, together with the bread size and crust type, if available, then press start once you have closed the lid of the machine.
5. When the bread is ready, using oven mitts, remove the bread pan from the machine. Use a stainless spatula to extract the bread from the pan and place the bread on a metallic rack to cool off before slicing it.

Nutritional facts:

Calories: 134, Fat: 6.8g, Carbs: 4.2g, Protein: 12g, Sugar: 4.1g, Potassium: 95mg, Sodium: 232mg

9.10 Pepper Cheddar Bread

Preparation Time: *5 minutes*
Cook Time: *15 minutes*
Servings: 10

Ingredients:

- coconut flour - ½ cup (100g)
- black pepper powder - 1 tsp (5g)
- almond blanched fine flour- 1 cup (130g)
- cheese of cheddar grated- 1 cup (130g)
- warm water- ¾ cup (150ml)
- Unsalted melted butter- 2 tsp (8.4g)
- Salt - 1 tsp (5g)
- active dry yeast - 1 tsp (5g)
- Baking powder - 1 tsp (5g)

Preparation:

1. Get a container for mixing, and combine the almond flour, coconut flour, shredded cheddar cheese, black pepper powder, baking powder, and salt.
2. Get another container, where you will combine the warm water and unsalted melted butter.
3. As per the instructions on the manual of your machine, pour the ingredients in the bread pan, taking care to follow how to mix in the yeast.
4. Put the bread pan in the machine, and select the basic bread setting, together with the bread size and crust type, if available, then press start once you have closed the lid of the machine.
5. When the bread is ready, using oven mitts, remove the bread pan from the machine.
6. Use a stainless spatula to extract the bread from the pan and place the bread on a metallic rack to cool off before slicing it.

Nutritional facts: Calories: 84, Fat: 4g, Carbs: 3g, Protein: 1g, Sugar: 1g, Potassium: 29mg, Sodium: 132mg

9.11 Olive Cheese Bread

Preparation Time: *5 minutes*
Cook Time: *40 minutes*
Servings: 6

Ingredients:

- Almond flour, 1 cup (120g)
- olives black halved - 1 cup (130g)
- olives green halved- 1 cup (130g)
- coconut flour - 1/3 cup (41g)
- active dry yeast - 1 tsp (5g)
- baking powder - 1 tsp (5g)
- shredded mozzarella cheese- 2/3 cup (227g)
- almond milk, unsweetened- 1/3 cup (113ml)
- melted unsalted butter - ¼ cups (59g)
- mayonnaise - 1/3 cup (113g)
- chopped green onions- ¼ cups (59g)

Preparation:

1. In a mixing container, combine the almond flour, coconut flour, shredded mozzarella cheese, chopped green onions, chopped black olives, chopped green olives, and baking powder.
2. Prepare another mixing container, where you will combine the unsweetened almond milk, mayonnaise, and melted unsalted butter.
3. As per the instructions on the manual of your machine, pour the ingredients in the bread pan, taking care to follow how to mix in the yeast.
4. Put the bread pan in the machine, and select the basic bread setting, together with the bread size and crust type, if available, then press start once you have closed the lid of the machine.

5. When the bread is ready, extract it and place it on a metallic mesh surface to cool completely before cutting and eating it.

Nutritional facts:

Calories: 182, Fat: 11g, Carbs: 14g, Protein: 2g, Sugar: 2.1g, Potassium: 97mg, Sodium: 278mg

9.12 Cheese Swirl Loaf

Preparation Time: 15 Minutes
Cook Time: 25 Minutes
Servings: 8
Ingredients:

- all-purpose flour - 3 cups (360g)
- sugar- 2 tbsp (30g)
- lukewarm milk- 1 1/4 cup (260g)
- melted butter- 2 tbsp (30g)
- salt- 1 tsp (5g)
- Monterey cheese- 4 slices
- instant yeast - 1 1/2 tsp (8.4g)
- edam or any quick melting cheese - 1/2 cup (100g)
- mozzarella cheese - 1/2 cup (100g)
- paprika- 1/2 tsp (2.84g).

Preparation:

1. Place all ingredients, except cheeses, in the bread pan in the liquid-dry-yeast layering.
2. Put the pan in the bread machine.
3. Select the Bake cycle.Choose Regular Basic Setting. Press start.
4. Place all the cheese in a microwavable bowl. Melt in the microwave for 30 seconds. Cool, but make sure to keep soft.
5. After 10 minutes into the kneading process, pause the machine. Take out half of the dough. Roll it flat on the work surface.
6. Spread the cheese on the flat dough, then roll it thinly. Return to the bread pan carefully.
7. Resume and wait until the loaf is cooked.
8. The machine will start the keep warm cycle after the bread is complete.

9. Let it stay in that mode for about 10 minutes before unplugging.
10. To end by removing the pan and let it cool down for about 10 minutes.

Nutritional facts:

Calories: 174, Fat: 3g, Carbs: 31g, Protein: 5g, Sugar: 2g, Potassium: 88mg, Sodium: 211mg

9.13 Goat Cheese Bread

Preparation Time: *5 minutes*
Cook Time: *40 minutes*
Servings: 6

Ingredients:

- almond blanched fine flour - 1 cup (130g)
- salt - ¼ tsp (2.4g)
- soy flour - ½ cup (100g)
- coconut milk, melted- ½ cup (100ml)
- fresh thyme, crushed- 2 tsp (8.4g)
- eggs- 2
- pepper cayenne - 1 tsp (5g)
- crumbled fresh goat cheese- 1 cup (130g)
- extra virgin olive oil- 1/3 cup (113ml)
- Dijon mustard - 1 tsp (5g)
- baking powder- 1 tsp (5g)
- active dry yeast - 1 tsp (5g)

Preparation:

1. Get a mixing container and combine the almond flour, soy flour, fresh thyme, cayenne pepper, salt, crumbled fresh goat cheese, and baking powder.
2. Get another mixing container and combine extra virgin olive oil, eggs, coconut milk, and Dijon mustard.
3. As per the instructions on the manual of your machine, pour the ingredients in the bread pan, taking care to follow how to mix in the yeast.

4. Put the bread pan in the machine, and select the basic bread setting, together with the bread size and crust type, if available, then press start once you have closed the lid of the machine.
5. When the bread is ready, using oven mitts, remove the bread pan from the machine. Use a stainless spatula to extract the bread from the pan and place the bread on a metallic rack to cool off before slicing it.

Nutritional facts:

Calories: 261, Fat: 20g, Carbs: 3g, Protein: 5g, Sugar: 8g, Potassium: 77mg, Sodium: 345mg

9.14 Blue Cheese Onion Bread

Preparation Time: *5 minutes*
Cook Time: *20 minutes*
Servings: 3

Ingredients:

- blue cheese, crumbled- ½ cup (100g)
- fresh rosemary, chopped - 2 tsp (8.4g)
- unsalted melted butter - 1 tsp (5g)
- Olive oil extra virgin - 2 tsp (8.4ml)
- almond fine flour - 1 ½ cup (100g)
- warm water - ½ cup (100ml)
- Baking powder- 1 tsp (5g)
- garlic cloves, crushed - 2
- yellow onion sliced and sautéed in butter until golden brown - 1
- Swerve sweetener - 1 tsp (5g)
- yeast - 1 tsp (5g)
- salt - 1 tsp (5g)

Preparation:

1. Prepare a mixing container, where you will combine the almond flour, Swerve sweetener, baking powder, freshly chopped rosemary, crumbled blue cheese, sautéed

sliced onion, salt, and crushed garlic.

2. Get another container, where you will combine the warm water, melted butter, and extra virgin olive oil.

3. As per the instructions on the manual of your machine, pour the ingredients in the bread pan, taking care to follow how to mix in the yeast.

4. Put the bread pan in the machine, and select the basic bread setting, together with the bread size and crust type, if available, then press start once you have closed the lid of the machine.

5. When the bread is ready, using oven mitts, remove the bread pan from the machine. Use a stainless spatula to extract the bread from the pan and place the bread on a metallic rack to cool off before slicing it.

Nutritional facts:

Calories: 182, Fat: 9g, Carbs: 14g, Protein: 5g, Sugar: 2g, Potassium: 87mg, Sodium: 282mg

9.15 Cheese Buttermilk Bread

Preparation Time: 5 Minutes
Cook Time: 2 Hours
Servings: 10
Ingredients:

- Buttermilk- 1 1/8 cups (266ml)
- Cheddar cheese- ¾ cup (150g)., shredded
- Active dry yeast- 1 ½ tsp (2.8g)
- Bread flour- 3 cups (360g)
- Sugar- 1 ½ tsp (8.8g)
- Salt- 1 1/2 tsp (8.4g)

Preparation:

1 Place all ingredients into the bread machine pan based on the bread machine manufacturer's instructions.

2 Select basic bread setting, then choose light/medium crust and start.

3 Once the loaf is ready, take out the loaf pan from the machine.
4 Allow it to cool for 10 minutes.
5 Slice and serve.

Nutritional facts:

Calories: 182, Fat: 3g, Carbs: 20g, Protein: 6g, Sugar: 2g, Potassium: 86mg, Sodium: 234mg

9.16 Cheese Pepperoni Bread

Preparation Time: 5 Minutes
Cook Time: 2 Hours
Servings: 10
Ingredients:

- Pepperoni- 2/3 cup (227g), diced
- Bread flour- 3 ¼ cups (477g)
- Active dry yeast- 1 ½ tsp (2.8g)
- Garlic salt - 1 ½ tsp (2.8g)
- Dried oregano - 1 ½ tsp (2.8g)
- Mozzarella cheese- 1/3 cup (113g)., shredded
- Sugar- 2 tbsp (30g)
- Warm water- 1 cup (130ml)+2 tbsp (30ml)

Preparation:

1 Add all ingredients except for pepperoni into the bread machine pan.
2 Select basic setting, then select medium crust and press start.
3 Add pepperoni just before the final kneading cycle.
4 Once the loaf is done, remove the loaf pan from the machine.
5 Allow it to cool for 10 minutes.
6 Slice and serve.

Nutritional facts: Calories: 176, Fat: 1.5g, Carbs: 34g, Protein: 5g, Sugar: 1g, Potassium: 27mg, Sodium: 387mg

10 SPICE BREAD

10.1 Anise Lemon Bread

Preparation Time: 2 hours
Cook Time: 15 minutes
Servings: 8
Ingredients:

- honey- 2⅔ tbsp (38g)
- butter, melted and cooled- 2⅔ tbsp (38g)
- lemon zest- 2/3 Tsp (3g)
- water, 2/3 Cup (158ml) at 80°F to 90°F (26 degree C to 32 degree C)
- egg, at room temperature- 1
- salt- 1/3 tsp (1.67g)
- anise seed- 2/3 Tsp (3g)
- white bread flour- 2 cups (240g)
- bread machine or instant yeast- 1 1/3 tsp (5.67g)

Preparation:

1 According to the manufacturer's instructions, add the ingredients to your bread machine.
2 Program the machine for Basic/White bread, Choose light or medium crust and then tap Start.
3 Take the bucket out of the machine once the loaf is finished baking.
4 Give the bread five minutes to cool.
5 Remove the loaf from the bucket with a gentle shake, then turn it out onto a cooling rack.

Nutritional facts:
Calories: 158, Fat: 5g, Carbs: 27g, Protein: 4g, Sugar: 1g, Potassium: 79mg, Sodium: 131mg

10.2 Fragrant Herb Bread

Preparation Time: 10 minutes
Cook Time: 15 minutes
Servings: 8 slices
Ingredients:

- water, ¾ cup (177ml) at 80°F to 90°F (26 degree C to 32 degree C)
- sugar- 1 Tbsp (15g)
- melted butter, cooled- 1 Tbsp (15g)
- skim milk powder- 2 tbsp (28.3g)
- salt- ¾ tsp (3.7g)
- dried chives- 1 tsp (5g)
- dried thyme- 1 tsp (5g)
- dried oregano- 1/2 tsp (2.84g)
- bread machine or instant yeast- ¾ tsp (3.7g)
- white bread flour- 2 cups (240g)

Preparation:

1. According to the manufacturer's instructions, add the ingredients to your bread machine.
2. Program the machine for Basic/White bread, Choose light or medium crust and then tap Start.
3. Take the bucket out of the machine once the loaf is finished baking.
4. Cool the bread for five minutes.
5. Remove the loaf from the bucket with a gentle shake, then place it on a cooling rack.

Nutritional facts:

Calories: 141, Fat: 2g, Carbs: 27g, Protein: 4g, Sugar: 1g, Potassium: 79mg, Sodium: 215mg

10.3 Lovely Aromatic Lavender Bread

Preparation Time: 5 minutes
Cook Time: 2 hours and 45 minutes
Servings: 8 slices
Ingredients:

- Milk, ¾ cup (150ml) at 80 degrees F
- sugar - 1 Tbsp (15g)

- melted butter, cooled - 1 Tbsp (15g)

- salt - ¾ tsp (3.7g)

- lemon zest - ¼ tsp (8.4g)

- fresh lavender flower, chopped - 1 tsp (5g)

- white bread flour- 2 cups (240g)

- fresh thyme, chopped - ¼ tsp (8.4g)

- instant yeast - ¾ tsp (3.7g)

Preparation:

1. Carefully follow the manufacturer's instructions when adding the ingredients to your breadmaker.

2. Set the program of your bread machine to Basic/White Bread and set crust type to Medium.

3. Wait until the cycle completes.

4. After the loaf has finished baking, remove the bucket and allow the bread to cool for five minutes.

5. To remove the bread, gently shake the bucket.

Nutritional facts:
Calories: 144, Fat: 2g, Carbs: 27g, Protein: 4g, Sugar: 6g, Potassium: 83mg, Sodium: 211mg

10.4 Delicious Honey Lavender Bread

Preparation Time: 10 minutes
Cook Time: 3 hours and 25 minutes
Servings: 16 slices
Ingredients:

- wheat flour - 1½ cup (188g)

- fresh yeast - 1 tsp (5g)

- whole meal flour - 2 1/3 cup (292g)

- lavender - 1 tsp (5g)

- water - 1½ cup (188ml)

- salt - 1 tsp (5g)

- honey - 1½ tbsp (22ml)

Preparation:

1. Sift both types of flour in a bowl and mix.

2. Carefully follow the manufacturer's instructions when adding the ingredients to your breadmaker.

3. Set the program of your bread machine to Basic/White Bread and set crust type to Medium.

4. Wait until the cycle completes.

5. After the loaf has finished baking, remove the bucket and allow the bread to cool for five minutes.

6. To remove the bread, gently shake the bucket.

Nutritional facts: Calories: 226, Fat: 1g, Carbs: 46g, Protein: 7g, Sugar: 1g, Potassium: 86mg, Sodium: 321mg

10.5 Oregano Mozza-Cheese Bread

Preparation Time: 15 minutes
Cook Time: 3 hours and 15 minutes
Servings: 16 slices
Ingredients:

- (milk + egg) mixture- 1 cup (130g)
- flour- 2¼ cups (281g)
- mozzarella cheese- ½ cup (100g)
- sugar - 2 tbsp (28.3g)
- whole grain flour - ¾ cup (150g)
- oregano - 2 tsp (8.4g)
- salt- 1 tsp (5g)
- dry yeast- 1 1/2 tsp (8.4g)

Preparation:

1. Put the ingredients in your bread machine, carefully following the instructions of the manufacturer.

2. Set the program of your bread machine to Basic/White Bread and set crust type to Dark.

3. Wait until the cycle completes.

4. Once the loaf is ready, take the bucket out and let the bread cool for five minutes.

5. Lightly shake the bucket to take out the loaf.

Nutritional facts:
Calories: 209, Fat: 2g, Carbs: 40g, Protein: 67g, Sugar: 1g, Potassium: 90mg, Sodium: 282mg

10.6 Turmeric Bread

Preparation Time: 5 minutes
Cook Time: 3 hours
Servings: 14
Ingredients:

- dried yeast- 1 tsp (5g)
- turmeric powder - 1 tsp (5g)
- strong white flour - 4 cups (544g)
- olive oil - 2 Tbsp (30ml)
- beetroot powder - 2 tsp (8.4g)
- chili flakes- 1 tsp (5g)
- salt - 1.5 tsp (6g)
- water - 1 3/8 cup (325ml)

Preparation:

1. Add each ingredient to the bread machine in the order and at the temperature recommended by your bread machine manufacturer.

2. Close the lid, select the basic bread, medium crust setting on your bread machine and press start.

3. When the bread machine has finished baking, remove the bread and put it on a cooling rack.

Nutritional facts:

Calories: 129, Fat: 3g, Carbs: 24g, Protein: 2g, Sugar: 1g, Potassium: 65mg, Sodium: 212mg

10.7 Rosemary Bread

Preparation Time: 2 hours 10 minutes
Cook Time: 50 minutes
Servings: 1 loaf
Ingredients:

- Water, ¾ cup (150ml) + 1 Tbsp (15ml) at 80 degrees F
- sugar - 2 tsp (8.4g)
- melted butter, cooled- 1⅔ tbsp (18g)
- salt - 1 tsp (5g)
- fresh rosemary, chopped - 1 Tbsp (15g)
- instant yeast- 1 1/3 tsp (5.67g)
- white bread flour - 4 cups (544g)

Preparation:

1 Put the ingredients in your bread machine, carefully following the instructions of the manufacturer.
2 Set the program of your bread machine to Basic/White Bread and set crust type to Medium.
3 Press START.
4 Wait until the cycle completes.
5 Once the loaf is ready, take the bucket out and allow bread cool for 5 minutes.
6 Lightly shake the bucket to take out the loaf.
7 Transfer to a cooling rack, slice, and serve.

Nutritional facts:
Calories: 142, Fat: 3g, Carbs: 25g, Protein: 4g, Sugar: 1g, Potassium: 74mg, Sodium: 213mg

10.8 Cumin Bread

Preparation Time: 3 hours 30 minutes
Cook Time: 15 minutes
Servings: 8
Ingredients:

- bread machine flour, sifted - 1/3 cup (113g)
- sugar - 1½ Tbsp (24g)
- kosher salt – 1 1/2 tsp (6.84g)
- lukewarm water - 1¾ cup (414ml)
- black cumin- 1 Tbsp (15g)
- bread machine yeast- 1 Tbsp (15g)
- sunflower oil - 2 Tbsp (30ml)

Preparation:

1 Place all the dry and liquid ingredients in the pan and follow the instructions for your bread machine.
2 Set the baking program to BASIC and the crust type to MEDIUM.
3 If the dough is too dense or too wet, adjust the amount of flour and liquid in the recipe.
4 When the program has ended, take the pan out of the bread machine and let it cool for 5 minutes.
5 Shake the loaf out of the pan. If necessary, use a spatula.
6 Wrap the bread with a kitchen towel and set it aside for an hour. Otherwise, you can cool it on a wire rack.

Nutritional facts:
Calories: 368, Fat: 6g, Carbs: 67g, Protein: 69g, Sugar: 9g, Potassium: 127mg, Sodium: 444mg

10.9 Lavender Buttermilk Bread

Preparation Time: 10 minutes
Cook Time: 3 hours
Servings: 14
Ingredients:

- water - ½ cup (125ml)
- buttermilk- 7/8 cup (207ml)
- olive oil - 1/4 cup (21ml)
- finely chopped fresh lavender leaves- 3 Tbsp (42g)
- Grated zest of 1 lemon
- finely chopped fresh lavender flowers - 1 ¼ tsp (8.4g)
- bread flour - 4 cups (544g)
- bread machine yeast - 2 3/4 tsp (9g)
- salt - 2 tsp (8.4g)

Preparation:

1. Add each ingredient to the bread machine in the order and at the temperature recommended by your bread machine manufacturer.

2. Close the lid, select the basic bread, medium crust setting on your bread machine and press start.

3. When the bread machine has finished baking, remove the bread and put it on a cooling rack.

Nutritional facts:

Calories: 170, Fat: 5g, Carbs: 27g, Protein: 2g, Sugar: 3g, Potassium: 99mg, Sodium: 245mg

10.10 Cajun and Tomato Bread

Preparation Time: 2 hours
Cook Time: 15 minutes
Servings: 8
Ingredients:

- water, ¾ cup (177ml) at 80°F to 90°F (26 degree C to 32 degree C)
- tomato paste- 1 tsp (5g)
- melted butter, cooled- 1 Tbsp (15g)
- salt- 1 tsp (5g)
- sugar- 1 Tbsp (15g)
- Cajun seasoning- ½ tbsp (7g)
- skim milk powder- 3 Tbsp (42g)
- white bread flour- 3 cups (360g)
- onion powder- ⅛ tsp (3g)
- bread machine or instant yeast- 1 tsp (5g)

Preparation:

1 As directed by the manufacturer, add the ingredients to your bread machine.
2 After setting the machine to make Basic/White bread, choose a light or medium crust and push Start.
3 After the loaf has finished baking, take the bucket out of the machine.
4 5 minutes should pass as the loaf cools.
5 To release the loaf, gently shake the bucket. Then, turn the loaf over onto a cooling rack.

Nutritional facts:

Calories: 141, Fat: 2g, Carbs: 27g, Protein: 4g, Sugar: 4g, Potassium: 97mg, Sodium: 215mg

10.11 Rosemary Cranberry Pecan Bread

Preparation Time: 30 minutes
Cook Time: 3 hours
Servings: 14
Ingredients:

- water, 1 1/3 cup (333ml) plus 2 Tbsp (30ml)
- butter- 2 Tbsp (30g)
- salt - 2 tsp (8.4g)
- bread flour - 4 cups (544g)
- dried sweetened cranberries - 3/4 cup (150g)
- non-fat powdered milk- 2 Tbsp (30g)
- toasted chopped pecans - 3/4 cup (150g)
- sugar - ¼ cups (59g)
- yeast - 2 tsp (8.4g)

Preparation:

1. Add each ingredient to the bread machine in the order and at the temperature recommended by your bread machine manufacturer.

2. Close the lid, select the basic bread, medium crust setting on your bread machine and press start.

3. When the bread machine has finished baking, remove the bread and put it on a cooling rack.

Nutritional facts:

Calories: 132, Fat: 5g, Carbs: 18g, Protein: 9g, Sugar: 3.89g, Potassium: 87mg, Sodium: 120mg

10.12 Chives Bread

Preparation Time: 3 hours 30 minutes
Cook Time: 15 minutes
Servings: 8
Ingredients:

- water, ¾ cup (177ml) at 80°F to 90°F (26 degree C to 32 degree C)
- sugar- 1 Tbsp (15g)
- melted butter, cooled- 1 Tbsp (15g)
- skim powder- 2 Tbsp (30g)
- salt- ¾ tsp (3.7g)
- garlic powder- 1/2 tsp (2.84g)
- minced chives- 1 Tbsp (15g)
- white bread flour- 3 cups (360g)
- cracked black pepper- 1/2 tsp (2.84g)
- bread machine or instant yeast- ¾ tsp (3.7g)

Preparation:

1 Follow the manufacturer's instructions when adding the ingredients to your bread machine.
2 Set the machine to produce basic/white bread. After choosing a light or medium crust, tap Start.
3 Take the bucket out of the machine once the loaf is finished baking.
4 Give the bread five minutes to cool.
5 Remove the loaf from the bucket with a gentle shake, then turn it out onto a cooling rack.

Nutritional facts:
Calories: 141, Fat: 2g, Carbs: 27g, Protein: 4g, Sugar: 1g, Potassium: 27mg, Sodium: 215mg

10.13 Saffron Tomato Bread

Preparation Time: 3 hours 30 minutes
Cook Time: 15 minutes
Servings: 10
Ingredients:

- bread machine yeast - 1 tsp (5g)
- panifarin - 1 Tbsp (15g)
- wheat bread machine flour - 2½ cup (313g)
- white sugar- 1½ Tbsp (23g)
- kosher salt – 1 1/2 tsp (6.84g)
- tomatoes, dried and chopped - 1 Tbsp (15g)
- extra-virgin olive oil - 2 Tbsp (30ml)
- firm cheese (cubes)- 1 Tbsp (15g)
- tomato paste - 1 Tbsp (15g)
- feta cheese - ½ cup (100g)
- serum- 1½ cup (188g)
- saffron - 1 pinch

Preparation:

1. Five minutes before cooking, pour in dried tomatoes and 1 Tbsp (15g) of olive oil. Add the tomato paste and mix.
2. Place all the dry and liquid ingredients, except additives, in the pan and follow the instructions for your bread machine.
3. Pay particular attention to measuring the ingredients. Use a measuring cup, measuring spoon, and kitchen scales to do so.
4. Set the baking program to BASIC and the crust type to MEDIUM.
5. Add the additives after the beep or place them in the dispenser of the bread machine.
6. Shake the loaf out of the pan. If necessary, use a spatula.
7. Wrap the bread with a kitchen towel and set it aside for an hour. Otherwise, you can cool it on a wire rack.

Nutritional facts:
Calories: 260, Fat: 9g, Carbs: 35g, Protein: 8g, Sugar: 5g, Potassium: 145mg, Sodium: 611mg

10.14 Potato Rosemary Loaf

Preparation Time: 5 minutes
Cook Time: 3 hours and 25 minutes
Servings: 20 slices
Ingredients:

- wheat flour - 4 cups (544g)
- sunflower oil - 1 Tbsp (15ml)
- sugar - 1 Tbsp (15g)
- water - 1½ cup (375ml)
- salt – 1 1/2 tsp (8.4g)
- dry yeast - 1 tsp (5g)
- crushed rosemary to taste
- mashed potatoes, ground through a sieve - 1 cup (130g)

Preparation:

1. Add flour, salt, and sugar to the bread machine bucket and attach mixing paddle.

2. Add sunflower oil and water.

3. Put in yeast as directed.

4. Set the program of your bread machine to Bread with Filling mode and set crust type to Medium.

5. Once the bread machine beeps and signals to add more ingredients, open lid, add mashed potatoes, and chopped rosemary.

6. Wait until the cycle completes.

7. Once the loaf is ready, take the bucket out and allow loaf cool for 5 minutes.

8. Lightly shake the bucket to take out the loaf.

Nutritional facts:
Calories: 276, Fat: 3g, Carbs: 54g, Protein: 8g, Sugar: 1g, Potassium: 60mg, Sodium: 372mg

10.15 Cardamon Bread

Preparation Time: 2 hours
Cook Time: 15 minutes
Servings: 8
Ingredients:

- milk, ½ cup (125ml) at 80°F to 90°F (26 degree C to 32 degree C)
- egg, at room temperature- 1
- honey- 2 tsp (8.4ml)
- ground cardamom- 2/3 Tsp (3g)
- salt- 2/3 Tsp (3g)
- white bread flour- 3 cups (360g)
- melted butter, cooled- 1 tsp (5g)
- bread machine or instant yeast- ¾ tsp (3.7g)

Preparation:

1. According to the manufacturer's instructions, add the ingredients to your bread machine.
2. Set the breadmaker to make basic/white bread. Tap Start after selecting a light or medium crust.
3. Take the bucket out of the machine once the loaf is finished baking.
4. Give the bread five minutes to cool.
5. Remove the loaf from the bucket with a gentle shake, then turn it out onto a cooling rack.

Nutritional facts:
Calories: 149, Fat: 2g, Carbs: 29g, Protein: 5g, Sugar: 4g, Potassium: 76mg, Sodium: 211mg

10.16 Cumin Tossed Fancy Bread

Nutritional facts: Calories: 368, Fat: 7g, Carbs: 67g, Protein: 9g, Sugar: 1g, Potassium: 89mg, Sodium: 192mg

Preparation Time: 5 minutes
Cook Time: 3 hours and 15 minutes
Servings: 16 slices
Ingredients:

- wheat flour - 5 1/3 cup (670g)

- sugar - 1½ tbsp (22g)

- salt – 1 1/2 tsp (8.4g)

- dry yeast - 1 Tbsp (15g)

- water - 1¾ cup (270ml)

- sunflower oil- 3 Tbsp (42g)

- cumin - 2 Tbsp (28.3g)

Preparation:

1. Add warm water to the bread machine bucket.

2. Add salt, sugar, and sunflower oil.

3. Sift in wheat flour and add yeast.

4. Set the program of your bread machine to French bread and set crust type to Medium.

5. Once the maker beeps, add cumin.

6. Wait until the cycle completes.

7. Once the loaf is ready, take the bucket out and let the loaf cool for 5 minutes.

8. Lightly shake the bucket to take out the loaf.

11 HERB BREAD

11.1 Caramelized Onion Bread

Preparation Time: *15 minutes*

Cook Time: 3 hours 35 minutes

Servings: 14 slices

Ingredients:

- butter - ½ tbsp (7g)
- water - 1 cup (130ml)
- onions, ½ cup (100g) sliced
- Gold Medal Better for Bread flour- 3 cups (360g)
- olive oil - 1 Tbsp (15ml)
- salt - 1 tsp (5g)
- Sugar- 2 Tbsp (30g)
- bread machine or quick active dry yeast - 1 ¼ tsp (8.4g)

Preparation:

1. Dissolve the butter over medium-low heat in a skillet.
2. Cook the onions in the butter for 10 to 15 minutes until they are brown and caramelized—then remove from the heat.
3. Add each ingredient except the onions to the bread machine in the order and at the temperature recommended by your bread machine manufacturer.
4. Close the lid, select the basic bread, medium crust setting on your bread machine, and press Start.
5. Add ½ cup (100g) of onions 5 to 10 minutes before the last kneading cycle ends.
6. When the bread machine has finished baking, remove the bread and put it on a cooling rack.

Nutritional facts: Calories: 160, Fat: 3g, Carbs: 30g, Protein: 4g, Sugar: 2g, Potassium: 27mg, Sodium: 192mg

11.2 Olive Bread

Preparation Time: *10 minutes*

Cook Time: *3 hours*

Servings: 14 slices

Ingredients:

- Brine from olive jar- ½ cup (100ml)
- Olive oil- 2 Tbsp (30ml)
- Warm water 43 degree C (110°F) to make 1 ½ cup (375ml) when combined with brine
- Bread flour- 3 cups (360g)
- Salt- 1 1/2 tsp (6.84g)
- Whole wheat flour- 1 2/3 cup (227g)
- Sugar- 2 Tbsp (30g) (28.3g)
- Dried leaf basil- 1 1/2 tsp (6.84g)
- Active dry yeast- 2 tsp (8.4g)
- Finely chopped kalamata olives- 2/3 cup (227g)

Preparation:

1. Add each ingredient except the olives to the bread machine in the order and at the temperature recommended by your bread machine manufacturer.
2. Close the lid, select the wheat, medium crust setting on your bread machine, and click Start.
3. Add the olives 10 minutes before the last kneading cycle ends.
4. When the bread machine has finished baking, remove the bread and put it on a cooling rack.

Nutritional facts: Calories: 141, Fat: 2g, Carbs: 29g, Protein: 5g, Sugar: 1g, Potassium: 89mg, Sodium: 245mg

11.3 Dilly Onion Bread

Preparation Time: *10 minutes*

Cook Time: 3 hours and 5 minutes

Servings: 14 slices

Ingredients:

- Water- ¾ cup (150ml) 70°F (21 degrees C)
- Sugar- 2 Tbsp (30g)
- Butter, softened- 1 Tbsp (15g)
- Dried parsley flakes- 2 Tbsp (30g)
- Dried minced onion- 3 Tbsp (42g)
- Salt- 1 tsp (5g)
- Dill weed- 1 Tbsp (15g)
- Bread flour- 2 cups (240g)
- Garlic clove, minced- 1
- Nonfat dry milk powder- 1 Tbsp (15g)
- Whole wheat flour- 1/3 cup (113g)
- Active dry yeast serving- 2 tsp (8.4g)

Preparation:

1. Add each ingredient to the bread machine in the order and at the temperature recommended by your bread machine manufacturer.
2. Close the lid, select the basic bread, medium crust setting on your bread machine, and press Start.
3. When the bread machine has finished baking, remove the bread and put it on a cooling rack.

Nutritional facts: Calories: 78, Fat: 1g, Carbs: 17g, Protein: 3g, Sugar: 1g, Potassium: 27mg, Sodium: 192mg

11.4 Cardamom Cranberry Bread

Preparation Time: *5 minutes*

Cook Time: *3 hours*

Servings: 14 slices

Ingredients:

- Water- 1¾ cup (270ml)
- Salt- 1 1/2 tsp (6.84g)
- Brown sugar- 2 Tbsp (30g)
- Flour- 4 cups (544g)
- Coconut oil- 2 Tbsp (30g)
- Cardamom- 2 tsp (8.4g)
- Cinnamon- 2 tsp (8.4g)
- Yeast- 2 tsp (8.4g)
- Dried cranberries- 1 cup (130g)

Preparation:

1. Add each ingredient except the dried cranberries to the bread machine in the order and at the temperature recommended by your bread machine manufacturer.
2. Close the lid, select the basic bread, medium crust setting on your bread machine, and press Start.
3. Add the dried cranberries 5 to 10 minutes before the last kneading cycle ends.
4. When the bread machine has finished baking, remove the bread and put it on a cooling rack.

Nutritional facts:

Calories: 157, Fat: 3g, Carbs: 4g, Protein: 3g, Sugar: 2g, Potassium: 27mg, Sodium: 272mg

11.5 Original Italian Herb Bread

Preparation Time: 2 hours 40 minutes
Cook Time: 50 minutes
Servings: 2 loaves
Ingredients:

- Water at 80 degrees F (26 degrees C)- 1 cup (237ml)
- Butter- 1½ tbsp (22g)
- Olive brine- ½ cup (100ml)
- Salt- 1 tsp (5g)
- Sugar- 3 Tbsp (42g)
- Flour- 5 1/3 cup (675g)
- Bread machine yeast- 1 tsp (5g)
- Olives, black/green- 20
- Italian herbs- 1 1/2 tsp (8.4g)

Preparation:

1. Cut olives into slices.
2. Put the ingredients in your bread machine (except olives), carefully following the instructions of the manufacturer.
3. Set the program of your bread machine to French bread and set crust type to Medium.
4. Press START.
5. Once the maker beeps, add olives.
6. Wait until the cycle completes.
7. Once the loaf is ready, take the bucket out and allow loaf cool for 5 minutes.
8. Lightly shake the bucket to take out the loaf.
9. Transfer to a cooling rack, slice, and serve.

Nutritional facts:

Calories: 386, Fat: 7g, Carbs: 71g, Protein: 10g, Sugar: 1g, Potassium: 156mg, Sodium: 592mg

11.6 Herbed Pesto Bread

Preparation Time: 5 minutes
Cook Time: 50 minutes
Servings: 8 slices
Ingredients:

- water, 2/3 cup (158ml) at 80°F to 90°F (26 degree C to 32 degree C)
- minced garlic- 1 tsp (5g)
- melted butter, cooled- 1½ tbsp (22g)
- salt- ¾ tsp (3.7g)
- sugar- ½ tbsp (7g)
- chopped fresh basil- ¾ tsp (3.7g)
- chopped fresh parsley- 2 Tbsp (30g)
- white bread flour- 2 cups (240g)
- grated Parmesan cheese- ¼ cups (59g)
- bread machine or active dry yeast- ¾ tsp (3.7g)

Preparation:

1. As directed by the manufacturer, add the ingredients to your breadmaker.
2. Select a light or medium crust, program the machine for Basic/White bread, and then click Start.
3. After the loaf has finished baking, take the bucket out of the machine.
4. Give the bread five minutes to cool.
5. Remove the loaf from the bucket with a gentle shake, then turn it out onto a cooling rack.

Nutritional facts:

Calories: 149, Fat: 3g, Carbs: 25g, Protein: 5g, Sugar: 0.23g, Potassium: 56mg, Sodium: 243mg

11.7 Chive Bread

Preparation Time: *10 minutes*
Cook Time: *3 hours*
Servings: 14 slices

Ingredients:

- milk (70°F) 21 degrees C- ¾ tsp (3.7ml)
- sour cream- ¼ cups (59g)
- water (70°F) 21 degrees C- ¼ cups (59ml)
- sugar -1 1/2 tsp (2.84g)
- butter - 2 Tbsp (30g)
- bread flour- 3 cups (360g)
- salt - 1 1/2 tsp (2.84g)
- minced chives- ¼ cups (59g)
- baking soda - ⅛ tsp (1.2g)
- active dry yeast leaves - 2 ¼ tsp (8.4g)

Preparation:

1. Add each ingredient to the bread machine in the order and at the temperature recommended by your bread machine manufacturer.
2. Close the lid, select the basic bread, medium crust setting on your bread machine, and press Start.
3. When the bread machine has finished baking, remove the bread and put it on a cooling rack.

Nutritional facts:

Calories: 105, Fat: 18g, Carbs: 18g, Protein: 4g, Sugar: 2g, Potassium: 87mg, Sodium: 282mg

11.8 Pumpkin Cinnamon Bread

Preparation Time: *10 minutes*
Cook Time: *3 hours*
Servings: 14 slices

Ingredients:

- canned pumpkin- 1 cup (130g)
- eggs- 2
- vanilla- 1 tsp (5g)
- baking powder- 2 tsp (8.4g)
- all-purpose bread flour- 1 ½ cup (188g)
- vegetable oil - 1/3 cup (113ml)
- salt - ¼ tsp (8.4g)
- ground nutmeg- ¼ tsp (8.4g)
- ground cloves- ⅛ tsp (2.84g)
- sugar - 1 cup (130g)
- ground cinnamon - ¼ tsp (8.4g)

Preparation:

1. Add each ingredient to the bread machine in the order and at the temperature recommended by your bread machine manufacturer.
2. Close the lid, select the quick, medium crust setting on your bread machine, and click Start.
3. When the bread machine has finished baking, remove the bread and put it on a cooling rack.

Nutritional facts:

Calories: 140, Fat: 5g, Carbs: 39g, Protein: 3g, Sugar: 5g, Potassium: 46mg, Sodium: 282mg

11.9 Garlic Bread

Preparation Time: 2 hours 30 minutes
Cook Time: 40 minutes
Servings: 1 loaf

Ingredients:
- Water- 1 3/8 cups (325ml)
- minced garlic- 1 tsp (5g)
- olive oil- 1 Tbsp (15ml)
- white sugar- 2 Tbsp (30g)
- bread flour- 2 cups (240g)
- salt- 1 tsp (5g)
- dried basil- 1 tsp (5g)
- grated Parmesan cheese- 1/4 cup (21g)
- chopped fresh chives- 2 Tbsp (30g)
- garlic powder- 1 tsp (5g)
- coarsely ground black pepper- 1 tsp (5g)
- bread machine yeast- 1/2 tsp (8.4g)

Preparation:

1. Follow the order of putting the ingredients into the pan of the bread machine recommended by the manufacturer.

2. Choose the Basic or the White Bread cycle on the machine and press the Start button.

Nutritional facts:
Calories: 175, Fat: 3g, Carbs: 29g, Protein: 5g, Sugar: 2g, Potassium: 107mg, Sodium: 332mg

11.10 Inspiring Cinnamon Bread

Preparation Time: 15 minutes
Cook Time: 2 hours and 15 minutes
Servings: 8 slices
Ingredients:

- Milk, 2/3 cup (158ml) at 80 degrees F (26 degrees C)
- melted butter, cooled - 3 Tbsp (42g)
- whole egg, beaten- 1
- salt - 1/3 tsp (15g)
- sugar- 1/3 cup (113g)
- white bread flour - 2 cups (240g)
- ground cinnamon - 1 tsp (5g)
- active dry yeast - 1 1/3 tsp (15g)

Preparation:

1. Put the ingredients to your bread machine, carefully following the instructions of the manufacturer.

2. Set the program of your bread machine to Basic/White Bread and set crust type to Medium.

3. Wait until the cycle completes.

4. Once the loaf is ready, take the bucket out and allow the loaf to cool for 5 minutes.

5. Remove the loaf.

Nutritional facts: Calories: 198, Fat: 5g, Carbs: 34g, Protein: 5g, Sugar: 5g, Potassium: 84mg, Sodium: 321mg

11.11 Herbal Garlic Cream Cheese Delight

Preparation Time: 5 minutes
Cook Time: 2 hours and 45 minutes
Servings: 8 slices
Ingredients:

- Water, 1/3 cup (113ml) at 80 degrees F (26 degrees C)
- whole egg, beaten, at room temp- 1
- herb and garlic cream cheese mix, at room temp- 1/3 cup (113g)
- sugar- 1 Tbsp (15g)
- melted butter, cooled - 4 tsp (24ml)
- white bread flour - 2 cups (240g)
- salt - 2/3 tsp (15g)
- instant yeast - 1 tsp (5g)

Preparation:

1. Put the ingredients in your bread machine, carefully following the instructions of the manufacturer.

2. Set the program of your bread machine to Basic/White Bread and set crust type to Medium.

3. Wait until the cycle completes.

4. Once the loaf is ready, take the bucket out and allow loaf to cool for 5 minutes.

5. Lightly shake the bucket to take out the loaf.

Nutritional facts:
Calories: 182, Fat: 6g, Carbs: 27g, Protein: 5g, Sugar: 1g, Potassium: 27mg, Sodium: 242mg

11.12 Dill And Rosemary Herb Bread

Preparation Time: 1 hour 20 minutes
Cook Time: 50 minutes
Servings: 1 loaf
Ingredients:
- Milk- 3/4 cup (177ml)
- Salt- 1 tsp (5g)
- Sugar- 1 Tbsp (15g)
- chopped onion- 1/3 cup (113g)
- butter or margarine- 1 Tbsp (15g)
- Dried dill- 1/2 tsp (2.84g)
- bread flour- 3 cups (360g)
- Dried rosemary- 1/2 tsp (8.4g)
- Dried basil- 1/2 tsp (8.4g)
- Active dry yeast - 1 1/2 tsp (8g)

Preparation:

1. Place the ingredients in the bread pan. Select medium crus then the rapid bake cycle. Press starts.

2. After 5-10 minutes, observe the dough as it kneads, if you hear straining sounds in your machine or if the dough appears stiff and dry, add 1 Tbsp (15g) Liquid at a time until the dough becomes smooth, pliable, soft, and slightly tacky to the touch.

3. Take out the bread from the pan after baking. Place on rack and allow to cool for 1 hour before slicing.

Nutritional facts:
Calories: 66, Fat: 0g, Carbs: 15g, Protein: 2g, Sugar: 1g, Potassium: 27mg, Sodium: 192mg

11.13 Sesame French Bread

Preparation Time: 20 minutes
Cook Time: 3 hours 15 minutes
Servings: 14
Ingredients:
- water - 7/8 cup (207ml)
- bread flour - 3 cups (360g)
- butter, softened- 1 Tbsp (15g)
- salt - 1 tsp (5g)
- sugar - 2 tsp (8.4g)
- sesame seeds toasted - 2 Tbsp (30g)
- yeast - 2 tsp (8.4g)

Preparation:

1. Add each ingredient to the bread machine in the order and at the temperature recommended by your bread machine manufacturer.

2. Close the lid, select the French bread, medium crust setting on your bread machine and press start.

3. When the bread machine has finished baking, remove the bread and put it on a cooling rack.

Nutritional facts:

Calories: 180, Fat: 3g, Carbs: 28g, Protein: 6g, Sugar: 3g, Potassium: 68mg, Sodium: 290mg

11.14 Cinnamon & Dried Fruits Bread

Preparation Time: 5 minutes
Cook Time: 3 hours
Servings: 16 slices
Ingredients:

- flour - 2¾ cup (344g)
- sugar - 4 tbsp (56g)
- dried fruits - 1½ cup (188g)
- milk powder - 1 Tbsp (15g)
- butter - 2½ tbsp (45g)
- ground nutmeg- 1/2 tsp (2.84g)
- cinnamon- 1 tsp (5g)
- peanuts - ½ cup (100g)
- vanillin - ¼ tsp (8.4g)
- salt - 1 tsp (5g)
- powdered sugar, for sprinkling
- bread machine yeast – 1 1/2 tsp (8g)

Preparation:

1. Put the ingredients in your bread machine (except peanuts and powdered sugar), carefully following the instructions of the manufacturer.

2. Set the program of your bread machine to Basic/White Bread and set crust type to Medium.

3. Once the bread machine beeps, moisten dough with a bit of water and add peanuts.

4. Wait until the cycle completes.

5. Once the loaf is ready, take the bucket out and allow bread cool for 5 minutes.

6. Lightly shake the bucket to take out the bread.

7. Sprinkle with powdered sugar.

Nutritional facts:

Calories: 315, Fat: 4g, Carbs: 65g, Protein: 5g, Sugar: 1g, Potassium: 124mg, Sodium: 492mg

11.15 Italian Ciabatta Bread

Preparation Time: *5 minutes*

Cook Time: 3 hours 5 minutes

Servings: 14 slices

Ingredients:

- margarine - 2 Tbsp (30g)
- water - 1 ½ cup (188ml)
- sugar - 2 Tbsp (30g)
- dried marjoram - 1 1/2 tsp (6.84g)
- powdered milk - 3 Tbsp (42g)
- salt - 1 1/2 tsp (6.84g)
- dried basil - 1 1/2 tsp (6.84g)
- yeast - 1 ¼ tsp (8.4g)
- bread flour- 4 cups (544g)
- dried thyme - 1 1/2 tsp (6.84g)

Preparation:

1. Add each ingredient to the bread machine in the order and at the

temperature recommended by your bread machine manufacturer.

2. Close the lid, select the basic bread, medium crust setting on your bread machine, and press Start.

3. When the bread machine has finished baking, remove the bread and put it on a cooling rack.

Nutritional facts:

Calories: 120, Fat: 3g, Carbs: 4g, Protein: 4g, Sugar: 2g, Potassium: 65mg, Sodium: 292mg

Nutritional facts: Calories: 151, Fat: 4g, Carbs: 24g, Protein: 5g, Sugar: 1g, Potassium: 66mg, Sodium: 234mg

11.16 Onion and Garlic Bread

Preparation Time: *10 minutes*

Cook Time: 2 hours 10 minutes

Servings: 14 slices

Ingredients:

- water - ½ cup (100ml)
- chopped green bell pepper - ¼ cups (59g)
- chopped onion - ¼ cups (59g)
- soft butter - 2 tsp (8.4g)
- finely chopped garlic- 2 tsp (8.4g)
- sugar - 1 Tbsp (15g)
- bread flour - 2 cups (240g)
- salt- 1/2 tsp (2.84g)
- Cajun - 1 tsp (5g)
- active dry yeast- 1 tsp (5g)

Preparation:

1. Add each ingredient to the bread machine in the order and at the temperature recommended by your bread machine manufacturer.

2. Close the lid, select the basic bread, medium crust setting on your bread machine, and press Start.

3. When the bread machine has finished baking, remove the bread and put it on a cooling rack.

12 VEGETABLE BREAD

12.1 Cauliflower and Garlic Bread

Preparation Time: 10 minutes

Cook Time: 4 hours

Servings: 9

Ingredients:

- eggs, 5 separated
- rice cauliflower - 1 1/2 cup (360g)
- coconut flour- 2/3 cup (227g)
- sea salt - 1/2 tsp (2.84g)
- garlic, minced- 1 tsp (5g)
- parsley, chopped - 1/2 Tbsp (30g)
- rosemary, chopped- 1/2 Tbsp (30g)
- unsalted butter- 3 Tbsp (42g)
- baking powder- 3/4 tbsp (56g)

Preparation:

1. Place the cauliflower rice in a bowl and cover it. Microwave for 3–4 minutes or until steaming. Then drain. Wrap in cheesecloth and remove as much moisture as possible. Set aside.

2. Place egg whites in a mixing container and whisk until stiff peaks form.

3. Then transfer 1/4 of the whipped egg whites into a food processor. Add remaining ingredients except for cauliflower and pulse for 2 minutes until blended.

4. Add cauliflower rice, and pulse for 2 minutes until combined. Then pulse in the remaining egg whites until just mixed.

5. Add batter into the bread bucket and cover. Select the BASIC/WHITE cycle. Press START.

6. Remove the bread when done. Cool, slice, and serve.

Nutritional facts:

Calories: 105, Fat: 6g, Carbs: 2g, Protein: 9g, Sugar: 1g, Potassium: 86mg, Sodium: 211mg

12.2 Vegetable Loaf

Preparation Time: 10 minutes

Cook Time: 4 hours

Servings: 12 slices

Ingredients:

- Eggs- 4
- medium zucchini, grated- 1
- coconut oil- 1/4 cup (21ml)
- small carrot, grated- 1
- pumpkin, grated - 1 cup (130g)
- almond flour- 1 cup (130g)
- coconut flour- 1/3 cup (113g)
- flaxseeds - 2 Tbsp (30g)
- sesame seeds- 2 Tbsp (30g)
- sunflower seeds- 2 Tbsp (30g)
- salt- 2 tsp (8.4g)
- psyllium husks- 2 Tbsp (30g)
- pumpkin seeds- 2 Tbsp (30g)
- cumin, ground- 2 tsp (8.4g)
- smoked paprika - 1 Tbsp (14g)
- baking powder - 2 tsp (8.4g)

Preparation:

1. Beat the eggs till frothy, beat in the oil, and then stir in zucchini, pumpkin, and carrot until just mixed. Place flour in another bowl. Then stir in the remaining ingredients until mixed.

2. Add egg mixture into the bread bucket, top with flour mixture, and cover.

3. Select the BASIC/WHITE cycle. Press START. Remove the bread when done. Cool, slice, and serve.

Nutritional facts:

Calories: 178, Fat: 12g, Carbs: 5g, Protein: 8g, Sugar: 1g, Potassium: 69mg, Sodium: 289mg

12.3 Almond Pumpkin Bread

Preparation Time: 10 minutes

Cook Time: 60 minutes

Servings: 16

Ingredients:

- oil - 1/3 cup (113ml)
- pumpkin puree, canned - 1 1/2 cup (360g)
- large eggs- 3
- baking powder - 1 1/2 tsp (8.4g)
- granulated sugar - 1 cup (130g)
- salt - 1/4 tsp (1.42g)
- baking soda- 1/2 tsp (2.84g)
- nutmeg, ground- 1/4 tsp (1.42g)
- cinnamon, ground- 3/4 tsp(3.42g)
- almond flour- 3 cups (360g)
- ginger, ground- 1/4 tsp (1.42g)
- pecans, chopped- 1/2 cup (100g)

Preparation:

1. Grease the bread machine pan with cooking spray. Stir all the wet ingredients in a bowl. Add all the dry ingredients except pecans until mixed.

2. Pour the batter onto the bread machine pan and place it back inside the bread machine. Close and select QUICK BREAD. Add the pecans after the beep. Remove the bread when done. Cool, slice, and serve.

Nutritional facts:

Calories: 52, Fat: 12g, Carbs: 5g, Protein: 11g, Sugar: 1g, Potassium: 57mg, Sodium: 126mg

12.4 Celery Bread

Preparation Time: 10 minutes

Cook Time: 3 hours

Servings: 1 loaf
Ingredients:

- cream of celery soup- 1 can 10 oz (283g)
- vegetable oil- 1 Tbsp (14ml)
- low-fat milk, heated- 3 Tbsp (42ml)
- celery, fresh, sliced thin- 3/4 cup (150g)
- celery, garlic, or onion salt- 1 1/4 tsp (1.42g)
- egg- 1
- celery leaves, fresh and chopped - 1 Tbsp (14g)
- sugar- 1/4 tsp (1.42g)
- bread flour- 3 cups (360g)
- ginger- 1/4 tsp (1.42g)
- quick-cooking oats- 1/2 cup (100g)
- gluten- 2 Tbsp (30g)
- celery seeds- 2 tsp (8.4g)
- active dry yeast- 1 package

Preparation:

1. Add all ingredients to the bread machine. Select the basic bread setting.

2. Remove the bread when done. Cool, slice, and serve.

Nutritional facts:

Calories: 70, Fat: 2g, Carbs: 7g, Protein: 4g, Sugar: 1g, Potassium: 27mg, Sodium: 125mg

12.5 Keto Almond Bread

Preparation Time: 25 minutes

Cook Time: 2 hours

Servings: 12

Ingredients:

- water - 1 1/2 cup (320ml)
- unsalted butter- 2 Tbsp (30g)+2 tsp (8.4g)
- salt- 1 1/2 tsp (8.4g)
- sugar- 1 Tbsp (14g)+1 tsp (5g)
- non-fat dry milk- 2 Tbsp (30ml)+2 tsp (8.4ml)
- almond flour- 4 cups (544g)
- active dry yeast - 2 tsp (8.4g)
- dry onion soup mix - 4 tbsp (56g)

Preparation:

1. Add all ingredients except dry onion soup mix in the bread machine pan.

2. Close the lid. Select BASIC cycle on the bread machine and then press START.

3. The machine will ping after around 30–40 minutes.

4. Pause the bread machine and add the dry onion soup mix.

5. Press START again and allow the cycle to continue. Once the loaf is finished, transfer it to a cooling rack.

6. Slice and serve with cream cheese or butter or as a soup side dish.

Nutritional facts:

Calories: 326, Fat: 14g, Carbs: 38g, Protein: 7g, Sugar: 1g, Potassium: 54mg, Sodium: 492mg

12.6 Sundried Tomato Bread

Preparation Time: 10 minutes

Cook Time: 2 hours

Servings: 10

Ingredients:

- flour - 2 1/4 cup (21g)
- kosher salt - 1 tsp (5g)
- baking powder - 1 Tbsp (14g)
- buttermilk- 1 1/2 cup (320ml)
- large eggs- 3
- basil, dried- 1 Tbsp (14g)
- canola oil - 6 tbsp (85ml)
- Sundried Tomato Roughly, Chopped- 1 cup (130g)

Preparation:

1. Place all the fixings in the bread machine bucket except for basil and sundried tomato.

2. Secure the lid cover. Select the QUICK BREAD setting on the bread machine, then press START.

3. Wait for the ping, fruit, and nut signal to open the lid, and add the basil and sundried tomato. Place a cover and press START to continue. When the cycle finishes, transfer the loaf to a wire rack and let it cool.

4. Slice and serve.

Nutritional facts:

Calories: 180, Fat: 4g, Carbs: 30g, Protein: 3g, Sugar: 1g, Potassium: 97mg, Sodium: 234mg

12.7 Onion Bread

Preparation Time: 20 minutes

Cook Time: 5 minutes

Servings: 6

Ingredients:

- Red onion, 1 diced and sautéed with 1/2 tsp (2.84g) butter until golden brown
- salt - 1/4 tsp (1.42g)
- unsalted butter, melted- 3 tsp (15g)
- psyllium husk flour - 3 tsp (15g)
- garlic, ground - 1/4 tsp (1.42g)
- baking powder- 1/2 tsp (2.84g)
- eggs - 5
- onion powder- 1/2 tsp (2.84g)
- active dry yeast - 3/4 tsp (3.84g)
- flour - 1 cup (130g)

Preparation:

1. Get a mixing container and combine the flour, salt, psyllium husk flour, ground onion, baking powder, and ground garlic.

2. Get another mixing container and mix the melted unsalted butter, eggs, and sautéed onions.

3. As per the instructions in the machine manual, pour the ingredients into the bread pan and follow the yeast instructions.

4. Put bread pan in the machine, and select the basic bread setting - together with the bread size and crust type if available - then press start once you have closed the lid of the machine.

5. When the bread is ready, extract it, and place it on a metallic mesh surface to cool completely before cutting and eating it.

Nutritional facts:

Calories: 124, Fat: 9g, Carbs: 1g, Protein: 9g, Sugar: 1g, Potassium: 78mg, Sodium: 211mg

12.8 Tomato Bread

Preparation Time: 15 minutes

Cook Time: 45 minutes

Servings: 16 Slices

Ingredients:

- whole eggs- 4
- flaxseed meal - 1 cup (130g)
- salted butter, melted- 2 Tbsp (30g)
- baking powder - 2 tsp (8.4g)
- oat fiber - 4 tsp *(16g)*
- sea salt - 1/4 tsp (1.42g)
- xanthan gum- 1 1/2 tsp (6.84g)
- garlic powder- 1/4 tsp (1.42g)
- basil, dried- 1/2 tsp (2.84g)
- parmesan, grated- 1/4 cup (21g)
- sun-dried tomatoes, diced- 2 Tbsp (30g)

Preparation:

1. Carefully whisk eggs and butter together. Pour all the ingredients into the bread machine pan.

2. Close the lid. Set the bread machine program to CAKE for 30–45 minutes (depending on the bread machine model) and choose the crust color LIGHT. Press START. Help the bread machine knead the dough with a spatula, if necessary. Before the baking cycle begins, sprinkle the top with grated parmesan.

3. After baking for 20 minutes, check for doneness with a toothpick. Wait until the program is complete, then take the bucket out and let it cool for 5–10 minutes.

4. Shake the loaf from the pan and let it cool for 30 minutes on a cooling rack.

5. Slice and serve.

Nutritional facts:

Calories: 87, Fat: 5.1g, Carbs: 2.2g, Protein: 3g, Sugar: 1g, Potassium: 27mg, Sodium: 112mg

12.9 Beetroot Bread

Preparation Time: 30 minutes

Cook Time: 45 minutes

Servings: 2

Ingredients:

- fresh beetroot, grated- 1 cup (130g)
- coconut flour- 1/2 cup (100g)
- almond flour - 1 cup (130g)
- cinnamon, ground- 1/4 tsp (1.42g)
- nutmeg, ground- 1/2 tsp (2.84g)
- Swerve sweetener- 1/3 cup (113g)
- active dry yeast- 2 tsp (8.4g)
- unsalted butter, melted- 4 tsp
- warm water - 1/2 cup (125ml)
- baking powder - 1 tsp (5g)
- walnuts, roasted and sliced- 1/3 cup (113g)
- salt - 1/4 tsp (1.42g)

Preparation:

1. Get a mixing container and combine the almond flour, coconut flour, roasted walnuts, Swerve sweetener, cinnamon ground, nutmeg powder, and baking powder.

2. Get another container and combine the warm water, shredded beetroot, and melted unsalted butter.

3. As per the instructions in the machine manual, pour the ingredients in the bread pan, taking care to follow how to mix in the yeast.

4. In the machine, place the bread pan, select the sweet bread setting - together with the crust type if available - then press start once you have closed the lid of the machine.

5. When the bread is ready, remove the bread pan from the machine using oven mitts. Use a stainless spatula to extract the bread from the pan and place the bread on a metallic rack to cool before slicing it.

Nutritional facts:

Calories: 852, Fat: 41g, Carbs: 43g, Protein: 23g, Sugar: 11g, Potassium: 227mg, Sodium: 1192mg

12.10 Carrot Bread

Preparation Time: 2h 10 Mins

Servings: 1 loaf / 8 slices

Ingredients:

- eggs - 4
- butter- ½ cup (100g)
- kosher salt - ¼ tsp (8.4g)
- vanilla sugar- 1 Tbsp (15g)
- sugar- ½ cup (100g)
- all-purpose flour - 3 cups (360g)
- cinnamon - 2 tsp (8.4g)
- ground nuts - ¼ cups (59g)
- baking powder- 1 Tbsp (15g)
- carrot, grated - ¾ cup (150g)

Preparation:

1. Follow the manufacturer's instructions and put all the ingredients into the bread machine (except the carrot). Set the program of the bread machine to CAKE/SWEET and set the crust type to LIGHT.

2. Press START. Once the machine beeps, add a grated carrot. When the cycle is completed, take the bucket out and allow bread cool for 5 minutes.

3. Shake the bucket gently to extract the loaf, then transfer to a cooling rack, slice, and serve. Enjoy!

Nutritional facts:

Calories: 395, Fat: 15g, Carbs: 52g, Protein: 10g, Sugar: 1g, Potassium: 102mg, Sodium: 492mg

12.11 Zucchini Bread

Preparation Time: 2h 10 Mins

Servings: 1 loaf / 8 slices

Ingredients:

- Eggs- 2
- oil - 1 cup (130ml)
- salt - ¼ tsp (8.4g)
- vanilla sugar - 1 Tbsp (15g)
- white sugar- 1 cup (130g)
- nuts, ground - ½ cup (100g)
- cinnamon - 2 tsp (8.4g)
- baking powder- 1 Tbsp (15g)
- all-purpose flour, well sifted- 3 cups (360g)
- Zucchini, Grated- 1¼ cups (59g)

Preparation:

1. Follow the manufacturer's instructions and put the ingredients in the bread machine (except the zucchini).

2. Set the program of the bread machine to CAKE/SWEET and set the crust type to LIGHT.

3. Press START. Once the machine beeps, add zucchini. When the cycle is completed, take the bucket out and allow bread cool for 5 minutes.

4. Shake the bucket gently to take out the loaf, then transfer to a cooling rack, slice, and serve.

Nutritional facts:

Calories: 555, Fat: 30g, Carbs: 62g, Protein: 9g, Sugar: 1g, Potassium: 127mg, Sodium: 322mg

12.12 Pumpkin Bread

Preparation Time: 10 minutes

Cook Time: 4 hours

Servings: 12 slices

Ingredients:

- eggs, pasteurized- 2
- sugar - 2/3 cup (227g)
- butter- 1 cup (130g)
- cloves, ground- 1/8 tsp (0.61g)
- pumpkin puree- 2/3 cup (227g)
- ginger, ground- 1/8 tsp (0.61g)
- cinnamon, ground- 1/2 tsp (2.84g)
- nutmeg, ground- 1/2 tsp (2.84g)
- baking powder - 1 tsp (5g)

Preparation:

1. Take a large bowl, crack eggs, and then beat the remaining ingredients in the order described in the ingredients until incorporated.

2. Add batter into the bread bucket, shut the lid, select the basic/white cycle setting and then press the UP/DOWN arrow button to adjust baking time according to the bread machine; it will take 3–4 hours.

3. Then press the crust button to select light crust if available, and press the START/STOP button to switch on the bread machine.

4. When the bread machine beeps, open the lid, take out the bread basket, and lift the bread.

5. Let bread cool on for one hour, then cut it into 12 slices and serve.

Nutritional facts: Calories: 148, Fat: 12g, Carbs: 7g, Protein: 6g, Sugar: 1g, Potassium: 89mg, Sodium: 321mg

13 MEAT BREAD

13.1 Ham Bread

Preparation Time: 30-45 minutes
Cook Time: 2 hours
Servings: 8
Ingredients:

- wheat flour - 3 1/3 cup (400g)
- milk powder- ½ cup (100g)
- ham- 1 cup (130g)
- fresh yeast- 1 tsp (5g)
- sugar - 1 ½ tbsp
- dried basil- 1 tsp (5g)
- salt - 1 tsp (5g)
- olive oil- 2 Tbsp (30g)
- water - 1 1/3 cup (333g)

Preparation:

1. Cut ham into cubes of 0.5-1 cm (approximately ¼ inch).
2. Put all ingredients in the bread machine from the following order: water, olive oil, salt, sugar, flour, milk powder, ham, and yeast.
3. Put all the ingredients according to the instructions in your bread machine.
4. Basil put in a dispenser or fill it later, at the signal in the container.
5. Turn on the bread machine.
6. After the end of the baking cycle, leave the bread container In the bread machine to keep warm for 1 hour.
7. Then your delicious bread is ready!

Nutritional facts:

Calories: 287, Fat: 5g, Carbs: 47g, Protein: 11g, Sugar: 6g, Potassium: 167mg, Sodium: 557mg

13.2 Meat Bread

Preparation Time: 1 hour 30 minutes
Cook Time: 1 hour 30 minutes
Servings: 8
Ingredients:

- boiled chicken- 2 cups (240g)
- milk- 1 cup (250ml)
- dry yeast- 1 Tbsp (15g)
- flour- 3 cups (360g)
- sugar - 1 tsp (5g)
- egg - 1
- oil - 2 Tbsp (30ml)
- salt- ½ tbsp

Preparation:

1. Pre-cook the meat. You can use a leg or fillet.
2. Separate meat from the bone and cut it into small pieces.
3. Pour all ingredients into the bread machine according to the instructions.
4. Add chicken pieces now.
5. The program is Basic.
6. This bread is perfectly served with dill and butter.

Nutritional facts:

Calories: 283, Fat: 6g, Carbs: 38g, Protein: 17g, Sugar: 2g, Potassium: 127mg, Sodium: 484mg

13.3 Onion Bacon Bread

Preparation Time: 1 hour 30 minutes
Cook Time: 1 hour 30 minutes
Servings: 8
Ingredients:

- water - 1 ½ cup (375ml)
- dry yeast - 3 tsp (15g)
- sugar - 2 Tbsp (30g)
- flour- 4 ½ cup (640g)
- salt - 2 tsp (8.4g)
- egg - 1
- small onions, chopped- 3
- oil - 1 Tbsp (15ml)
- bacon - 1 cup (130g)

Preparation:

1. Cut the bacon.
2. Put all ingredients into the machine.
3. Set it to the Basic program.
4. Enjoy this tasty bread!

Nutritional facts:
Calories: 391, Fat: 9g, Carbs: 59g, Protein: 14g, Sugar: 4g, Potassium: 121mg, Sodium: 960mg

13.4 Sausage Bread

Preparation Time: 2 hours
Cook Time: 2 hours
Servings: 8
Ingredients:

- dry yeast - 1 1/2 tsp (6.84g)
- sugar- 1 tsp (5g)
- flour - 3 cups (360g)
- whey - 1 1/3 cup (340g)
- salt- 1 1/2 tsp (6.84g)
- chopped smoked sausage- 1 cup (130g)
- oil- 1 Tbsp (15ml)

Preparation:

1. Fold all the ingredients in the order that is recommended specifically for your model.
2. Set the required parameters for baking bread.
3. When ready, remove the delicious hot bread.

4. Wait until it cools down and enjoy sausage.

Nutritional facts:
Calories: 234, Fat: 5g, Carbs: 38g, Protein: 7g, Sugar: 2g, Potassium: 78mg, Sodium: 535mg

13.5 Cheese Sausage Bread

Preparation Time: 2 hours
Cook Time: 2 hours
Servings: 8
Ingredients:

- dry yeast - 1 tsp (5g)
- salt- 1 tsp (5g)
- flour - 3 ½ cup (438g)
- oil - 1 ½ tbsp (22ml)
- sugar - 1 Tbsp (15g)
- grated cheese - 2 Tbsp (30g)
- smoked sausage- 2 Tbsp (30g)
- water - 1 cup (130ml)
- chopped garlic- 1 Tbsp (15g)

Preparation:

1. Cut the sausage into small cubes.
2. Grate the cheese on a grater
3. Chop the garlic.
4. Add all ingredients to the machine according to the instructions.
5. Turn on the baking program and let it do the work.

Nutritional facts:
Calories: 260, Fat: 5g, Carbs: 43g, Protein: 7g, Sugar: 1.7g, Potassium: 112mg, Sodium: 334mg

13.6 Collards & Bacon Loaf

Preparation Time: 15 minutes
Cook Time: 15 minutes
Servings: 4
Ingredients:

- whole-wheat pizza dough- 1 lb (453g)
- thinly sliced cooked collard greens - 2 cups (240g)
- garlic-flavored olive oil - 3 Tbsp (42ml)
- crumbled cooked bacon- ¼ cups (59g)
- shredded Cheddar cheese- 1 cup (130g)

Preparation:

1. Heat grill to medium-high.

2. Roll out dough to an oval that's 12 inches on a surface that's lightly floured. Move to a big baking sheet that's lightly floured. Put Cheddar, collards, oil, and dough on the grill.

3. Grease grill rack. Move to grill the crust. Cover the lid and cook for 1-2 minutes until it becomes light brown and puffed.

4. Use tongs to flip over the crust—spread oil on the crust and top with Cheddar and collards. Close lid and cook until cheese melts for another 2-3 minutes or the crust is light brown at the bottom.

5. Put pizza on the baking sheet and top using bacon.

Nutritional facts: Calories: 498, Fat: 28g, Carbs: 50g, Protein: 19g, Sugar: 3g, Potassium: 122mg, Sodium: 573mg

14 SOURDOUGH BREADS

14.1 Honey Sourdough Bread

Preparation Time: *15 minutes*
Cook Time: *3 hours*
Servings: 1 loaf

Ingredients:

- sourdough starter- 2/3 cup (227g)
- vegetable oil - 1 Tbsp (15ml)
- water - ½ cup (125ml)
- salt- 1/2 tsp (2.84g)
- honey - 2 Tbsp (30ml)
- bread flour- 2 cups (240g)
- high protein wheat flour - ½ cup (100g)
- active dry yeast - 1 tsp (5g)

Preparation:

1. Measure 1 cup (130g) of starter and add the residual bread ingredients to the bread machine pan.

2. Choose the basic/white bread cycle with medium or light crust color.

Nutritional facts: Calories: 175, Fat: 0.3g, Carbs: 33g, Protein: 5.6g, Sugar: 1g, Potassium: 97mg, Sodium: 121mg

14.2 Multigrain Sourdough Bread

Preparation Time: *15 minutes*
Cook Time: *3 hours*
Servings: 1 loaf

Ingredients:

- sourdough starter- 2 cups (240g)
- milk - ½ cup (118ml)
- butter, 2 Tbsp (30g)or 2 Tbsp (30ml)olive oil
- honey - ¼ cups (59ml)
- salt - 1 tsp (5g)
- millet, ½ cup (100g) or ½ cup (100g) amaranth or ½ cup (100g) quinoa
- sunflower seeds - ½ cup (100g)
- multi-grain flour - 3 ½ cup (438g)

Preparation:

1. Add ingredients to the bread machine pan.
2. Choose the dough cycle.
3. When the cycle is over, take out dough and place on a lightly floured surface, and shape it into a loaf.
4. Put in a greased loaf pan, cover, and rise until the bread is a couple of inches above the edge.
5. For 40 to 50 minutes, bake at 375°F.

Nutritional facts: Calories: 110, Fat: 1.8g, Carbs: 13g, Protein: 2.7g, Sugar: 1g, Potassium: 76mg, Sodium: 213mg

14.3 Olive and Garlic Sourdough Bread

Preparation Time: 15 minutes; 1 week (starter)
Cook Time: 3 hours
Servings: 1 loaf
Ingredients:

- sourdough starter- 2 cups (240g)
- olive oil - 2 Tbsp (30ml)
- flour- 3 cups (360g)
- salt - 2 tsp (8.4g)
- sugar - 2 Tbsp (30g)
- chopped garlic - 6 cloves
- chopped black olives- ½ cup (100g)

Preparation:

1. Add the starter and bread ingredients to the bread machine pan.
2. Choose the dough cycle.
3. Preheat oven to 375°F(190 degrees C).
4. When the cycle is complete, if the dough is sticky, add more flour.
5. Shape dough onto a baking sheet or put into a loaf pan
6. Bake for 35-45 minutes until golden.

7. Cool before slicing.

Nutritional facts:

Calories: 150, Fat: 0.5g, Carbs: 26.5g, Protein: 3.4g, Sugar: 1g, Potassium: 78mg, Sodium: 267mg

14.4 Sourdough Boule

Preparation Time: 4 hours

Cook Time: 25-35 minutes

Servings: 12

Ingredients:

- warm water- 1 1/8 cup (275 ml)
- all-purpose flour- 4 cups (550 g)
- sourdough starter - 4 cups (500 g)
- salt- 1 ½ tbsp (20 g)

Preparation:

1. Combine the flour, warm water, and starter, and let it sit, covered for at least 30 minutes.
2. After letting it sit, stir in the salt, and turn dough out onto a surface dusted with flour. It should be sticky; you do not have to worry.
3. Flatten the dough slightly (it's best to "slap" it onto the counter), then fold it in half a few times.
4. Cover the dough and let it rise. Repeat the slap and fold a few more times. Now cover the dough and let it rise for 2-4 hours.
5. When the dough is at least doubles in size, gently pull it, so the top of the dough is exposed. Repeat several times. Let it rise for 2-4 hours once more.
6. Preheat to oven to 475°F (246 degrees C), and either place a baking stone or a cast iron pan in the oven to preheat.
7. Place the risen dough on the stone or pot, and score the top in several

spots. For 20 minutes, bake, then reduce the heat to 475°F (246 degrees C), and bake for 25-35 minutes more. The boule will be golden brown.

Nutritional facts:

Calories: 243, Fat: 0.7g, Carbs: 4g, Protein: 6.9g, Sugar: 1g, Potassium: 89mg, Sodium: 392mg

14.5 Herbed Baguette

Preparation Time: *45 minutes*

Cook Time: 20-25 minutes

Servings: 12

Ingredients:

- warm water - 1 ¼ cups (178ml)
- sourdough starter, either fed or unfed- 2 cups (240g)
- all-purpose flour- 4 to 5 cups (946g to 1182g)
- salt- 2 1/2 tsp (10.84g)
- sugar - 2 tsp (8.4g)
- instant yeast - 1 Tbsp (15g)
- fresh oregano, chopped- 1 Tbsp (15g)
- fresh rosemary, chopped- 1 tsp (5g)
- fresh basil, chopped- 1 Tbsp (15g)
- Any other desired herbs

Preparation:

1. In the bowl of a mixer, combine all the ingredients, knead with a dough hook (or use your hands) until a smooth dough is formed—about 7 to 10 minutes; if necessary, add more flour.
2. Oil a bowl and place the dough, cover, and let it rest for about 2 hours.
3. Beat the dough and divide it into 3 parts. Create each piece of dough into a loaf of bread, about 16 inches long. You can do this by rolling the

dough into a trunk, folding it, rolling it into a trunk, and then folding it again.

4. Place the rolled baguette dough onto lined baking sheets, and cover. Let it rise for one hour.
5. Preheat oven to 475°F (246 degrees C), and bake for 20-25 minutes

Nutritional facts:

Calories: 197, Fat: 0.6g, Carbs: 4g, Protein: 5g, Sugar: 1g, Potassium: 67mg, Sodium: 212mg

14.6 Czech Sourdough Bread

Preparation Time: 15 minutes
Cook Time: *3 hours*
Servings: 1 loaf

Ingredients:

- non-dairy milk- 1 cup (175ml)
- honey - 1 Tbsp (15ml)
- salt - 1 Tbsp (15g)
- rye flour - 1 ½ cup (188g)
- sourdough starter - 1 cup (130g)
- wheat flour- ¾ cup (150g)
- bread flour - 1 cup (130g)
- wheat gluten- 5 Tbsp (70g)
- grated half-baked potato - 1 ½ cup (200g)
- caraway seeds - 2 tsp (8.4g)

Preparation:

1. Fill the bread machine pan with the ingredients.
2. Decide on the dough cycle.
3. The dough should rise in the bread machine for up to 24 hours until it doubles in size. Bake in the bread machine for an hour after rising.

Nutritional facts: Calories: 132, Fat: 0.8g, Carbs: 4g, Protein: 6.5g, Sugar: 1g, Potassium: 89mg, Sodium: 888mg

14.7 Sauerkraut Rye

Preparation Time: 2 hours 20 minutes
Cook Time: 50 *minutes*
Servings: 1 loaf

Ingredients:

- sauerkraut, rinsed and drained- 1 cup (130g)
- molasses- 1½ tbsp (22g)
- warm water - ¾ cup (150ml)
- brown sugar- 1½ tbsp (22g)
- butter- 1½ tbsp (22g)
- salt – 1 1/2 tsp (8.4g)
- caraway seeds- 1 tsp (5g)
- bread flour- 2 cups (240g)
- rye flour- 1 cup (130g)
- active dry yeast- 1 1/2 tsp (8.4g)

Preparation:

1. Put all the ingredients to your bread machine.
2. Set the program of your bread machine to Basic/White Bread and set crust type to Medium.
3. Wait until the cycle completes.
4. Once the loaf is ready, take the bucket out and allow bread to cool for 5 minutes.
5. Lightly shake the bucket to take out the loaf.

Nutritional facts: Calories: 75, Fat: 2g, Carbs: 13g, Protein: 2g, Sugar: 1g, Potassium: 27mg, Sodium: 192mg

14.8 French Sourdough Bread

Preparation Time: 15 minutes
Cook Time: 3 *hours*
Servings: 2 loaf

Ingredients:

- sourdough starter- 2 cups (240g)
- water- ½ cup (125ml)
- salt - 1 tsp (5g)
- white cornmeal - 2 Tbsp (30g)
- white bread flour - 4 cups (544g)

Preparation:

1. Put the ingredients in the bread machine pan, saving cornmeal for later.
2. Choose the dough cycle.
3. Preheat oven to 375°F (190 degrees C).
4. At the end of the dough cycle, place dough onto a surface that is floured.
5. Add flour if the dough is sticky.
6. Divide dough into 2 portions and flatten it into an oval shape 1½ inch thick.
7. Fold ovals in half lengthwise and pinch seams to elongate.
8. Sprinkle cornmeal onto the baking sheet and place the loaves seam side down.
9. Cover and let it rise in until is about in doubled.
10. Place a deep pan of hot water on the bottom shelf of the oven
11. Use a knife to make shallow, diagonal slashes in the top of the loaves
12. Place the loaves in the oven and sprinkle with fine water. Spray the oven walls as well.
13. Repeat spraying 3 times at one-minute intervals.
14. Remove the pan of water after 15 minutes of baking
15. Fully bake for 30 to 40 minutes or till golden brown.

Nutritional facts: Calories: 937, Fat: 0.4g, Carbs: 196g, Protein: 26g, Sugar: 1g, Potassium: 178mg, Sodium: 1172mg

15 FRUIT BREAD

15.1 Banana Bread

Preparation Time: 1 hour 40 minutes

Cook Time: 40- 45 minutes

Servings: 1 loaf

Ingredients:

- Baking powder- 1 tsp (5g)

- bananas, peeled and halved lengthwise – 2

- Baking soda- 1/2 tsp (2.84g)

- eggs- 2

- all-purpose flour- 2 cups (240g)

- white sugar - 3/4 cup (150g)

- Vegetable oil - 3 tbsp (45ml)

Preparation:

1. Put all the ingredients in the bread pan—select dough setting. Start and mix for about 3-5 minutes.

2. After 3-5 minutes, press stop. Do not continue to mix. Smooth out the top of the dough

3. Using the spatula and then select bake, start and bake for about 50 minutes. After 50 minutes, insert a toothpick into the top center to test doneness.

4. Test the loaf again. When the bread is completely baked, take out pan from the machine and let the bread remain in the pan for ten minutes. Take out bread and cool on a wire rack.

Nutritional facts: Calories: 310, Fat: 13g, Carbs: 40g, Protein: 6g, Sugar: 1g, Potassium: 120mg, Sodium: 564mg

15.2 Orange and Walnut Bread

Preparation Time: 2 hours 50 minutes

Cook Time: 45 minutes

Servings: 10- 15

Ingredients:

- egg white- 1

- warm whey- ½ cup (100g)

- water- 1 Tbsp (15ml)

- sugar- 4 tbsp (60g)

- yeast- 1 Tbsp (15g)

- flour- 4 cups (544g)

- oranges, crushed- 2

- salt - 1 ½ tbsp (20g)

- salt- 1 tsp (5g)

- vanilla - 1/3 tsp (15g)

- orange peel- Three tsp

- Crushed pepper, salt, cheese for garnish

- walnut and almonds, crushed- 3 Tbsp (42g)

Preparation:

1. Put all of the ingredients in your Bread Machine (except egg white, 1 Tbsp (15g) water, and crushed pepper/ cheese).

2. Set the program to the "Dough" cycle and let the cycle run.

3. Remove the dough (using lightly floured hands) and carefully place it on a surface dusted with flour.

4. Conceal with a light film/cling paper and let the dough rise for 10 minutes.

5. Divide the dough into thirds after it has risen

6. Place on a lightly flour surface, roll each portion into 14x10 inch sized rectangles

7. Use a sharp knife to cut carefully cut the dough into strips of ½ inch width

8. Pick 2-3 strips and twist them multiple times, making sure to press the ends together

9. Preheat your oven to 400 degrees F(204 degrees C).

10. Take a bowl and stir egg white, water, and brush onto the breadsticks

11. Sprinkle salt, pepper/ cheese

12. Bake for 10-12 minutes till golden brown

13. Take out from the baking sheet, then place on a cooling rack. Serve and enjoy!

Nutritional facts:

Calories: 437, Fat: 7g, Carbs: 82g, Protein: 12g, Sugar: 1g, Potassium: 27mg, Sodium: 678mg

15.3 Apple with Pumpkin Bread

Preparation Time: 2 hours 50 minutes

Cook Time: 45 minutes

Servings: 2 loaves

Ingredients:

- dried apples, chopped- 1/3 cup (113g)

- almond flour - 4 cups (544g)

- bread machine yeast- 1 1/2 tsp (8g)

- ground nutmeg- 1/4 tsp (1.42g)

- ground pecans- 1/3 cup (113g)

- allspice- 1/4 tsp (1.42g)

- ground ginger - 1/4 tsp (1.42g)

- salt - 1 1/4 tsp (1.42g)

- ground cinnamon- 1/2 tsp (2.84g)

- dry skim milk powder- 1/3 cup (113g)

- unsalted butter, cubed - 2 Tbsp (30g)

- large eggs, at room temperature- 2

- honey- 1/4 cup (21g)

- water, 2/3 cup (227g) with a temperature of 80 to 90 degrees F (26 to 32 degrees C)

- pumpkin puree- 2/3 cup (227g)

Preparation:

1. Put all ingredients, excluding the dried apples, in the bread pan in this order: water, pumpkin puree, eggs, honey, skim milk, butter, salt, allspice, cinnamon, pecans, nutmeg, ginger, flour, and yeast.

2. Secure the pan in the machine and lock the lid.

3. Place the dried apples in the fruit and nut dispenser.

4. Turn on the machine. Choose the sweet setting and your desired color of the crust.

5. Carefully take out the baked bread once ready and leave it to cool for 20 minutes before slicing.

Nutritional facts:

Calories: 228, Fat: 4g, Carbs: 30g, Protein: 18g, Sugar: 1g, Potassium: 122mg, Sodium: 345mg

15.4 Date Delight Bread

Preparation Time: 2 hours

Cook Time: 15 minutes

Servings: 12

Ingredients:

- water, lukewarm- ¾ cup (177ml)

- butter, melted at room temperature - 2 Tbsp (30g)

- milk, lukewarm- ½ cup (125ml)

- molasses - 3 Tbsp (42g)

- honey - ¼ cups (59g)

- whole-wheat flour- 2 ¼ cups (340g)

- sugar- 1 Tbsp (15g)

- skim milk powder - 2 Tbsp (30g)

- white almond flour - One ¼ cups (59g)s

- salt- 1 tsp (5g)

- instant or bread machine yeast - 1 1/2 tsp (2.84g)

- unsweetened cocoa powder - 1 Tbsp (15g)

- chopped dates- ¾ cup (150g)

Preparation:

1. Take 1 ½ pound size loaf pan and add the liquid ingredients and then add the dry ingredients. (Do not add the dates as of now.)

2. Place the loaf pan in the machine and close its top lid.

3. Plug the bread machine into the power socket. For selecting a bread cycle, press "Basic Bread/White Bread/Regular Bread" or "Fruit/Nut Bread," and for choosing a crust type, press "Light" or "Medium."

4. Start the machine, and it will start preparing the bread. When the machine beeps or signals, add the dates.

5. After the bread loaf is completed, open the lid and take out the loaf pan.

6. Allow the pan to cool down for 10-15 minutes on a wire rack. Gently shake the pan and remove the bread loaf.

7. Make slices and serve.

Nutritional facts:

Calories: 220, Fat: 5g, Carbs: 52g, Protein: 6g, Sugar: 1g, Potassium: 87mg, Sodium: 321mg

15.5 Sun Vegetable Bread

Preparation Time: 15 minutes

Cook Time: 3 hours 45 minutes

Servings: 8 slices

Ingredients:

- wheat flour - 2 cups (250 g)

- panifarin- 2 tsp (8.4g)

- whole-wheat flour - 2 cups (250 g)

- salt – 1 1/2 tsp (8.4g)

- yeast- 2 tsp (8.4g)

- paprika dried slices - 1 Tbsp (15g)

- sugar - 1 Tbsp (15g)

- dried garlic- 1 Tbsp (15g)

- dried beets- 2 Tbsp (30g)

- vegetable oil - 1 Tbsp (15ml)

- water- 1½ cup (188ml)

Preparation:

1. Set baking program, which should be 4 hours; crust color is Medium.

2. Be sure to look at the kneading phase of the dough to get a smooth and soft bun.

Nutritional facts:

Calories: 253, Fat: 2.6g, Carbs: 49g, Protein: 7g, Sugar: 1g, Potassium: 179mg, Sodium: 444mg

15.6 Tomato Onion Bread

Preparation Time: 10 minutes

Cook Time: 3 hours 50 minutes

Servings: 12 slices

Ingredients:

- all-purpose flour - 2 cups (240g)

- warm water - ½ cup (100ml)

- whole meal flour- 1 cup (130g)

- olive oil - 3 Tbsp (42ml)

- milk - 4 3/4 ounces (140 ml)

- salt- 1 tsp (5g)

- sugar - 2 Tbsp (30g)

- baking powder - 1/2 tsp (2.84g)

- dry yeast - 2 tsp (8.4g)

- onion- 1

- sun-dried tomatoes- 5

- black pepper- ¼ tsp (8.4g)

Preparation:

1. Prepare all the necessary products. Finely chop the onion and sauté in a frying pan. Cut up the sun-dried tomatoes (10 halves).

2. Pour all liquid ingredients into the bowl; then cover with flour and put in the tomatoes and onions. Pour in the yeast and baking powder without touching the liquid.

3. Select the baking cycle and start. You can choose the Bread with Additives program, and then the bread machine will knead the dough at low speeds.

Nutritional facts:

Calories: 241, Fat: 6g, Carbs: 40g, Protein: 6g, Sugar: 1g, Potassium: 45mg, Sodium: 305mg

15.7 Fragrant Orange Bread

Preparation Time: 5 Minutes

Cook Time: 25 Minutes

Servings: 8

Ingredients:

- Milk- 1 cup (130ml)

- sugar- 3 Tbsp (42g)

- freshly clasped orange juice - 3 Tbsp (42ml)

- salt- 1 tsp (5g)

- melted butter cooled- 1 Tbsp (15g)

- Zest of 1 orange

- white almond flour- 3 cups (360g)

- bread machine or instant yeast - 1¼ tsp (7g)

Preparation:

1. Place the ingredients in your bread machine.

2. Select the Bake cycle. Select the light or medium crust option, set the machine to make white bread, and then click Start. When the loaf has finish baking, take the bucket out of the appliance. Allow the bread to cool for five minutes.

3. Moderately shake the pan to eliminate the loaf and put on a rack to cool.

Nutritional facts:

Calories: 277, Fat: 4g, Carbs: 48g, Protein: 9g, Sugar: 1g, Potassium: 87mg, Sodium: 321mg

15.8 Strawberry Shortcake Bread

Preparation Time: 10 Minutes

Cook Time: 25 Minutes

Servings: 8

Ingredients:

- milk, 1/2 cup (125ml) at 80°F to 90°F (26 degree C to 32 degree C)

- sugar- 3 Tbsp (42g)

- melted butter, cooled- 3 Tbsp (42g)

- sliced fresh strawberries - ¾ cup (150g)

- salt – 1 1/2 tsp (8.4g)

- quick oats - 1 cup (130g)

- bread machine or instant yeast- 1 1/2 tsp (8.4g)

- white almond flour - 2¼ cups (281g)

Preparation:

1. Fill the bread machine with the ingredients.

2. Select the Bake cycle. Choose a light or medium crust, program the machine for Whitbread, and then press Start.

3. Remove the bucket from the device after the bread is done.

4. Give the bread five minutes to cool. Remove the loaf from the can with a little shake and place it on a cooling rack.

Nutritional facts:

Calories: 277, Fat: 6g, Carbs: 48g, Protein: 9g, Sugar: 1g, Potassium: 86mg, Sodium: 300mg

15.9 Pineapple Coconut Bread

Preparation Time: 10 Minutes

Cook Time: 25 Minutes

Servings: 8

Ingredients:

- coconut milk- ½ cup (125ml)

- coconut extract – 1 1/2 tsp (8.4g)

- shredded sweetened coconut - ¾ cup (150g)

- butter, at room temperature - 6 tbsp (90g)

- all-purpose flour - 2 cups (240g)

- sugar- 1 cup (130g)

- salt- 1/2 tsp (2.84g)

- eggs- 2

- baking powder- 1 tsp (5g)

- pineapple juice- ½ cup (125ml)

Preparation:

1. Put the butter, eggs, coconut milk, pineapple juice, sugar, and coconut extract in the breadmaker.

2. Choosing the Bake cycle. Press Start after setting the machine to make Rapid bread. In a small bowl, combine the flour, coconut, baking soda, and salt as the wet ingredients are mixing.

3. After the first mixing and machine motions are finished, add the dry ingredients. When the loaf is ready, take the bucket out of the appliance. Allow the bread to cool for five minutes. Shake the machine slightly to release the bread and put on a rack to cool.

Nutritional facts:

Calories: 277, Fat: 8g, Carbs: 28g, Protein: 9g, Sugar: 1g, Potassium: 27mg, Sodium: 289mg

15.10 Fruit Syrup Bread

Preparation Time: 10 Minutes

Cook Time: 25 Minutes

Servings: 8

Ingredients:

- buckwheat flour - 3 2/3 cup (464g)

- unsalted butter, melted- 1/4 cup (21g)

- instant yeast- 1 1/2 tsp (2.84g)

- sugar - 2 Tbsp (30g)

- lukewarm water - 1 cup (125ml)

- rolled oats- 1/4 cup (21g)

- syrup from preserved fruit- 1/2 cup (100g)

- salt- 1/2 tsp (2.84g)

Preparation:

1. Combine the syrup and 1/2 cup (100ml) water. Heat until lukewarm. Add more water to precisely 1 cup (130ml) of water.

2. Place all the ingredients, except for the rolled oats and butter, in a liquid-dry-yeast layering.

3. Put the pan in the bread machine.

4. Load the rolled oats in the automatic dispenser.

5. Select the Bake cycle. Choose whole-wheat loaf.

6. Press start and wait until the loaf is cooked.

7. Brush the top with butter once cooked.

8. The machine will start the keep warm mode after the bread is complete.

9. Let it remain in that mode for about 10 minutes before unplugging.

10. Remove the pan and let it cool down for about 10 minutes.

Nutritional facts: Calories: 198, Fat: 6g, Carbs: 4g, Protein: 3g, Sugar: 1g, Potassium: 78mg, Sodium: 287mg

15.11 Lemon-Lime Blueberry Bread

Preparation Time: 10 Minutes

Cook Time: 25 Minutes

Servings: 8

Ingredients:

- plain yogurt at room temperature- ¾ cup (150g)

- honey- 3 Tbsp (42g)

- water - ½ cup (125ml)

- salt - 1 1/2 tsp (8.4g)

- melted butter cooled - 1 Tbsp (15g)

- lime zest - 1 tsp (5g)

- lemon extract- 1/2 tsp (2.84g)

- white almond flour - 3 cups (360g)

- dried blueberries - 1 cup (130g)

- bread machine or instant yeast- 2¼ tsp (8.4g)

Preparation:

1. Fill the bread machine with the ingredients.

2. Selecting the Bake cycle. Choose a light or medium crust, program the machine for Whitbread, and then press Start.

3. Take the bucket out of the machine.

4. Give the bread five minutes to cool.

5. Remove the loaf from the pan with a little shake and place it on a cooling rack.

Nutritional facts: Calories: 222, Fat: 5g, Carbs: 4g, Protein: 6g, Sugar: 1g, Potassium: 27mg, Sodium: 321mg

15.12 Cranberry Yogurt Bread

Preparation Time: 10 Minutes

Cook Time: 25 Minutes

Servings: 8

Ingredients:

- bread or all-purpose flour- 3 cups (360g) + 2 Tbsp (30g)

- olive or coconut oil - 1 Tbsp (14ml)

- lukewarm water - 1/2 cup (125ml)

- sugar- 3 Tbsp (42g)

- orange or lemon essential oil- 1 Tbsp (15ml)

- instant yeast- 2 tsp (8.4g)

- yogurt- 3/4 cup (150g)

- raisins- 1/2 cup (100g)

- dried cried cranberries - 1 cup (130g)

Preparation:

1. Place all ingredients, except cranberries and raisins, in the bread pan in the liquid-dry-yeast layering.

2. Put the pan in the bread machine.

3. Load the fruits in the automatic dispenser.

4. Select the Bake cycle. Choose White bread.

5. Press start and wait until the loaf is cooked.

6. The machine will start the keep warm mode after the bread is complete.

7. Allow it to stay in that mode for at least 10 minutes before unplugging.

8. Remove the pan and let it cool down for about 10 minutes.

Nutritional facts:

Calories: 234, Fat: 4g, Carbs: 4g, Protein: 2g, Sugar: 1g, Potassium: 76mg, Sodium: 311mg

16 SWEET BREAD

16.1 Lemon Poppy Seed Bread

Preparation Time: 10 minutes

Cook Time: 4 hours

Servings: 6

Ingredients:

- Eggs- 3
- lemon juice- 1 1/2 Tbsp (45g)
- unsalted butter, melted- 1 1/2 Tbsp (45g)
- almond flour - 1 1/2 cup (240g)
- lemon, zested- 1
- baking powder- 1/4 tsp (1.42g)
- erythritol sweetener - 1/4 cup (21g)
- poppy seeds- 1 Tbsp (14g)

Preparation:

1. Beat eggs, butter, lemon juice, and lemon zest until combined.

2. Add flour, sweetener, baking powder, and poppy seeds in another bowl and mix well.

3. Add the egg mixture to the bread pan, top with the flour mixture, and cover.

4. Select the BASIC/WHITE cycle and click START.

5. Remove the bread when done. Cool, slice, and serve.

Nutritional facts:

Calories: 200, Fat: 15g, Carbs: 2g, Protein: 9g, Sugar: 1g, Potassium: 111mg, Sodium: 321mg

16.2 Cinnamon Sweet Bread

Preparation Time: 10 minutes

Cook Time: 1 hour

Servings: 12

Ingredients:

- cinnamon, ground - 3 tsp (15g)
- large eggs-3
- almond flour- 1 1/2 cup (240g)
- vanilla essence- 1 tsp (5g)
- keto sweetener- 1/2 cup (100g)
- sour cream- 1/4 cup (21g)
- coconut flour - 1/4 cup (21g)
- almond milk, unsweetened - 1/2 cup (100g)
- baking powder - 1 tsp (5g)
- unsalted butter, melted - 1/2 cup (100g)

Preparation:

1. Put all ingredients into the bread machine.

2. Close the lid and choose the sweet bread cycle.

3. When cooking is over, remove the bread from the machine and let it rest for about 10 minutes.

Nutritional facts:

Calories: 190, Fat: 15g, Carbs: 4.5g, Protein: 7g, Sugar: 1g, Potassium: 78mg, Sodium: 256mg

16.3 Basic Sweet Yeast Bread

Preparation Time: 3 hours

Cook Time: 20 minutes

Servings: 8

Ingredients:

- Egg- 1
- sugar - 1/3 cup (113g)
- butter - 1/4 cup (21g)
- salt - 1/2 tsp (2.84g)
- milk- 1 cup (130ml)
- active dry yeast- 1 Tbsp (14g)
- flour- 4 cups (544g)

After beeping:

- Fruits/groundnuts

Preparation:

1. Put all ingredients in the bread machine, carefully following the instructions of the manufacturer (except fruits/groundnuts).

2. Set the program of the bread machine to basic/sweet and set the crust type to light or medium.

3. Press start. Once the machine beeps, add fruits/ground nuts.

4. When the cycle is completed, take the bucket out and allow bread cool for 5 minutes.

5. Shake the bucket gently to take out the loaf, then transfer to a cooling rack, slice, and serve.

Nutritional facts:

Calories: 336, Fat: 7g, Carbs: 2g, Protein: 9g, Sugar: 1g, Potassium: 123mg, Sodium: 456mg

16.4 Apricot Prune Bread

Preparation Time: 3 hours

Cook Time: 20 minutes

Servings: 8

Ingredients:

- Egg- 1
- apricot juice- 1/4 cup (21g)
- whole milk - 4/5 cup (200ml)
- sugar - 1/5 cup (282g)
- butter - 1/4 cup (21g)
- instant yeast- 1 Tbsp (14g)
- prunes, chopped - 5/8 cup (125g)
- salt- 1/4 tsp (1.42g)
- dried apricots, chopped - 5/8 cup (125g)

Preparation:

1. Put all ingredients into the bread machine, carefully following the manufacturer's instructions (except apricots and prunes).

2. Set the program of the bread machine to basic/sweet and set the crust type to light or medium.

3. Press start. Once the machine beeps, add apricots and prunes.

4. When the cycle is completed, take the bucket out and allow bread to cool for 5 minutes.

5. Shake the bucket gently to take out loaf, then transfer to a cooling rack, slice, and serve.

Nutritional facts:

Calories: 362, Fat: 6g, Carbs: 2g, Protein: 11g, Sugar: 1g, Potassium: 122mg, Sodium: 467mg

16.5 Citrus Bread

Preparation Time: 3 hours

Cook Time: 1 hour

Servings: 8

Ingredients:

- Egg- 1
- sugar - 1/3 cup (113g)
- butter - 3 Tbsp (42g).
- orange juice - 1/2 cup (125ml)
- vanilla sugar - 1 Tbsp (14g)
- salt - 1 tsp (5g)
- milk- 2/3 cup (227ml)
- instant yeast- 1 Tbsp (14g)
- almond flour- 4 cup
- lemon, candied - 1/4 cup (21g)
- oranges, candied- 1/4 cup (21g)
- Almonds, Chopped - 1/4 cup (21g)
- lemon zest - 2 tsp (8.4g)

Preparation:

1. Add the ingredients to the breadmaker, paying close attention to the manufacturer's instructions (except candied fruits, zest, and almonds).

2. Set the program of the bread machine to basic/sweet and set the crust type to light or medium.

3. Press start. Once the machine beeps, add candied fruits, lemon zest, and chopped almonds.

4. When the cycle is completed, take the bucket out and allow bread to cool for 5 minutes.

5. After removing the bread from the bucket with a light shake, place it on a cooling rack, slice it, and serve.

Nutritional facts:

Calories: 402, Fat: 7g, Carbs: 3g, Protein: 12g, Sugar: 1g, Potassium: 167mg, Sodium: 578mg

16.6 Fruit Bread

Preparation Time: 3 hours

Cook Time: 40 minutes

Servings: 8

Ingredients:

- Egg- 1
- Rum- 2 Tbsp (30g)
- Milk- 1 cup (130ml)
- brown sugar- 1/4 cup (21g)
- butter - 1/4 cup (21g)
- instant yeast - 1 Tbsp (14g)
- almond flour- 4 cups (544g)
- salt - 1 tsp (5g)

Fruits:

- dried apricots, coarsely chopped- 1/4 cup (21g)
- candied cherry, pitted- 1/4 cup (21g)
- prunes, coarsely chopped- 1/4 cup (21g)
- almonds, chopped- 1/4 cup (21g)
- seedless raisins- 1/2 cup (100g)

Preparation:

1. Put all ingredients in the bread machine, carefully following the instructions of the manufacturer (except fruits).

2. Set the program of the bread machine to basic/sweet and set crust type to light or medium. Click start. Once the machine beeps, add fruits. When the cycle is completed, take the bucket out and allow bread to cool for 5 minutes.

3. Shake the bucket gently to take out the bread, then transfer to a cooling rack, slice, and serve.

Nutritional facts:

Calories: 440, Fat: 8g, Carbs: 3g, Protein: 12g, Sugar: 1g, Potassium: 113mg, Sodium: 594mg

16.7 Marzipan Cherry Bread

Preparation Time: 3 hours

Cook Time: 35 minutes

Servings: 8

Ingredients:

- Egg- 1
- almond liqueur - 1 Tbsp (14g)
- Milk- 3/4 cup (150ml)
- ground almonds- 1/2 cup (100g)
- orange juice- 4 tbsp (56ml)
- sugar- 1/3 cup (113g)
- butter - 1/4 cup (21g)
- instant yeast- 1 Tbsp (14g)
- almond flour- 4 cups (544g)
- marzipan- 1/2 cup (100g)
- salt- 1 tsp (5g)
- dried cherries, pitted- 1/2 cup (100g)

Preparation:

1. Put all ingredients into the bread machine, carefully following the instructions of the manufacturer (except marzipan and cherry).

2. Set the program of the bread machine to basic/sweet and set the crust type to light or medium.

3. Press start.

4. Once the machine beeps, add marzipan and cherry. When the cycle is completed, take the bucket out and allow bread cool for 5 minutes.

5. Shake the bucket gently to take out bread, then transfer to a cooling rack, slice, and serve.

Nutritional facts:

Calories: 508, Fat: 14g, Carbs: 3g, Protein: 18g, Sugar: 1g, Potassium: 127mg, Sodium: 692mg

16.8 Raspberry Bread

Preparation Time: 10 minutes

Cook Time: 50 minutes

Servings: 12 slices

Ingredients:

- raspberries - 1 cup (130g)
- baking powder - 1 1/2 tsp (6.84g)
- sugar - 1/4 cup (21g)
- sour cream- 4 tbsp (56g)
- flour- 2 cups (240g)
- whole eggs- 2
- unsalted butter, melted- 4 tbsp (56g)
- lemon extract- 1 tsp (5g)
- vanilla- 1 tsp (5ml)
- lemon, juiced- 1/2

Preparation:

1. Put all the ingredients (except the raspberries) to the bread machine pan following the instructions for the device. Close the cover. Set the bread machine program to CAKE for 40–50 minutes.

2. After the signal, add the raspberries to the dough. Press START.

3. Check for doneness with a toothpick. The approximate baking time is 45 minutes.

4. Wait until the program is complete. When done, take the bucket out and let it cool for 10 minutes.

5. Shake the loaf from the pan and let it cool for 30 minutes on a cooling rack.

6. Slice and serve.

Nutritional facts:

Calories: 165, Fat: 12g, Carbs: 7g, Protein: 6g, Sugar: 1g, Potassium: 87mg, Sodium: 278mg

16.9 Blueberry Bread

Preparation Time: 10 minutes

Cook Time: 50 minutes

Servings: 12 slices

Ingredients:

- Blueberries- 1/2 cup (100g)
- baking powder - 2 tsp (8.4g)
- sugar - 1/3 cup (113g)
- sour cream- 4 tbsp (56g)
- flour - 2 cups (240g)
- whole eggs-2
- unsalted butter, melted - 4 tbsp (56g)
- vanilla- 1 tsp (5ml)

Preparation:

1. In a large container, beat eggs with an electric mixer well.

2. Pour them into the bread machine pan. Add all other ingredients. Close the lid.

3. Set the bread machine program to CAKE for 45–60 minutes (depending on the device).

4. Press START. After the signal indicating the beginning of the BAKE cycle, add the blueberries.

5. After 35 minutes of baking, start checking for doneness using a toothpick. The approximate baking time is 45–50 minutes. Wait until the program is complete. When done, take the bucket out and let it cool for 10 minutes.

6. Shake the loaf from the pan and let it cool for 30 minutes on a cooling rack.

7. Slice and serve.

Nutritional facts:

Calories: 163, Fat: 11g, Carbs: 10g, Protein: 4g, Sugar: 6g, Potassium: 68mg, Sodium: 235mg

16.10 Avocado Bread

Preparation Time: 10 minutes

Cook Time: 60–70 minutes

Servings: 14 slices

Ingredients:

- avocados, mashed- 4
- coconut flour - 1 cup (130g)
- almond flour- 2 cups (240g)
- avocado oil- 5 Tbsp (70ml)
- monk fruit sweetener - 1/2 cup (100g)
- kosher salt - 1/2 tsp (2.84g)
- cocoa powder, unsweetened- 4 tbsp (56g)
- vanilla extract- 1 tsp (5g)
- baking soda- 1 tsp (5g)
- chocolate chips - 1 cup (130g)

Preparation:

1. In a large bowl, mix all of the dry ingredients.

2. In a blender, combine all of the wet ingredients.

3. Put the wet ingredients into the bread machine pan.

4. Cover them with dry ingredients. Add half of the chocolate chips.

5. Close the cover. Set the bread machine program to CAKE. The time may differ depending on the device.

6. Press START. Help the machine to knead the dough, if necessary.

7. Before baking, top the bread with the remaining 1/2 cup (100g) of chocolate chips.

8. After 45 minutes of baking, start checking for doneness using a toothpick. The approximate baking time is 45–60 minutes. Wait until the program is complete.

9. When done, take the bucket out and let it cool for 10 minutes.

10. Shake the loaf from the pan and let it cool for 30 minutes on a cooling rack.

11. Slice and serve.

Nutritional facts:

Calories: 287, Fat: 22g, Carbs: 15g, Protein: 6g, Sugar: 3g, Potassium: 121mg, Sodium: 309mg

16.11 Gingerbread Cake

Preparation Time: 10 minutes

Cook Time: 45 minutes

Servings: 10 slices

Ingredients:

- large eggs- 4
- vanilla extract- 1 tsp (5g)
- butter, melted- 1/4 cup (21g)
- flour - 3/4 cup (150g)
- granulated sugar- 3/4 cup (150g)
- ginger, ground- 2 tsp (8.4g)
- baking powder- 1 tsp (5g)
- allspice, ground - 1/2 tsp (2.84g)
- cinnamon, ground- 2 tsp (8.4g)
- clove, ground- 1/2 tsp (2.84g)
- nutmeg, ground- 1/2 tsp (2.84g)
- kosher salt- 1/4 tsp (1.42g)

For the icing:

- vanilla extract - 1 tsp (5g)
- sugar- 1/4 cup (21g)

- walnuts, chopped- 1/4 cup (21g)
- cream cheese, softened- 1/2 cup (100g)

Preparation:

1. Whisk together the eggs, vanilla, and unsalted butter.

2. In a container, mix all the dry ingredients. Put the wet ingredients in the bread machine pan.

3. Cover them with dry ingredients. Close the lid.

4. Set the bread machine program to CAKE. The time may differ depending on the device.

5. Press START. After 30 minutes of baking, start checking for doneness using a toothpick. The approximate baking time is 40–45 minutes. Wait until the program is complete. When done, take the bucket out and let it cool for 10 minutes.

6. Shake the loaf from the pan and let it cool for 30 minutes on a cooling rack.

7. Slice and serve.

Nutritional facts:

Calories: 138, Fat: 4g, Carbs: 4g, Protein: 5g, Sugar: 2g, Potassium: 99mg, Sodium: 289mg

16.12 Lemon Bread

Preparation Time: *5 minutes*
Cook Time: 1 hour

Servings: *12 slices*
Ingredients:

- flour - 9.5 oz. (269g)
- sugar- 1/2 cup (100g)
- baking powder- 1/2 tsp (2.84g)
- lemons zest – *2*

- poppy seeds - 2 Tbsp (30g)
- butter, melted - 3 Tbsp (42g)
- lemon juice- 2 Tbsp (30ml)
- whole eggs - 6

For the Icing:

- sugar- 1/2 cup (100g)
- lemon juice - 1 Tbsp (14g)
- water- 2 Tbsp (30g)

Preparation:

1. Put all ingredients into the bread machine pan. Close the lid.

2. Set the bread machine program to CAKE. The time may differ depending on the device.

3. Press START. Help the machine to knead the dough, if necessary.

4. After 40 minutes of baking, start checking for doneness using a toothpick. The approximate baking time is 45–55 minutes.

5. Wait until the program is complete, and when done, take the bucket out and let it cool for 10 minutes.

6. Shake the loaf from the pan and let it cool for 30 minutes on a cooling rack.

7. Make the icing in a small bowl, mixing all the ingredients. Drizzle it over the bread.

8. Slice and serve.

Nutritional facts:

Calories: 191, Fat: 15g, Carbs: 14g, Protein: 6g, Sugar: 5g, Potassium: 67mg, Sodium: 234mg

17 GLUTEN-FREE BREAD

17.1 Gluten-free Pumpkin Pie Bread

Preparation Time: *5 minutes*
Cook Time: 2 hours 50 minutes

Servings: *12 slices*

Ingredients:

- olive oil- 1/4 cup (59ml)
- bourbon vanilla extract- 1 Tbsp (15g)
- large eggs, beaten- 2
- honey - 4 tbsp (56g)
- canned pumpkin- 1 cup (130g)
- buckwheat flour - 1/2 cup (100g)
- lemon juice - 1/4 tsp (1.42g)
- sorghum flour - 1/4 cup (21g)
- millet flour- 1/4 cup (21g)
- light brown sugar- 1 cup (130g)
- tapioca starch - 1/2 cup (100g)
- baking soda - 1 tsp (5g)
- baking powder - 2 tsp (8.4g)
- xanthan gum - 1 tsp (5g)
- sea salt- 1/2 tsp (2.84g)
- allspice - 1 tsp (5g)
- ground cinnamon - 1 tsp (5g)
- peach juice- 1-2 Tbsp (30ml)

Preparation:

1. In a bowl, combine the dry ingredients and set them aside.
2. Add the moist ingredients to the pan, excluding the peach juice.
3. Fill the bread maker's pan with the dry ingredients.
4. Click Start after selecting the Sweet bread cycle and choosing a light or medium crust color.
5. As the ingredients begin to combine, scrape down the edges with a delicate silicone spatula.
6. If the batter is too stiff, add peach juice 1 Tbsp at a time until the batter is similar in consistency to muffin batter.
7. Put the lid on and bake the meal. Put on a cooling rack for 20 minutes before slicing.

Nutritional facts:

Calories: 180, Fat: 5g, Carbs: 33g, Protein: 6g, Sugar: 5g, Potassium: 98mg, Sodium: 299mg

17.2 Gluten-free Pull-apart Rolls

Preparation Time: *5 minutes*
Cook Time: 2 hours

Servings: *9 slices*

Ingredients:

- warm water - 1 cup (130ml)
- Egg, room temperature- 1
- butter, unsalted - 2 Tbsp (30g)
- gluten-free almond-blend flour- 2 3/4 cup (390g)
- xanthan gum- 1 1/2 tsp (8.4g)
- apple cider vinegar - 1 tsp (5g)
- salt - 1 tsp (5g)
- Sugar- 1/4 cup (21g)
- active dry yeast- 2 tsp (8.4g)

Preparation:

1. Add the wet ingredients to the pan of the breadmaker.
2. Combine the dry ingredients in a pan, omitting the yeast.
3. Insert the yeast into the center of the dry ingredients.
4. Click Start after selecting the Dough cycle.

5. Spray nonstick cooking spray into an 8-inch round cake pan.
6. As soon as the dough cycle is over, split the dough into nine balls, place the balls in a cake pan, and thoroughly moisten the balls with warm water.
7. Put the ingredients in a warm place and cover with a cloth to allow it rise for an hour.
8. Set the oven to 400°F (204 degrees c).
9. Bake for 26 to 28 minutes, or until the top is golden.
10. Serve after brushing with butter.

Nutritional facts:

Calories: 568, Fat: 10g, Carbs: 46g, Protein: 6g, Sugar: 1g, Potassium: 156mg, Sodium: 657mg

17.3 Gluten-free Whole Grain Bread

Preparation Time: *5 minutes*

Cook Time: 3 hours 40 minutes

Servings: *12 slices*

Ingredients:

- sorghum flour- 2/3 cup (227g)
- millet flour - 1/2 cup (100g)
- buckwheat flour- 1/2 cup (100g)
- xanthan gum- 2 1/4 tsp (1.42g)
- potato starch- 3/4 cup (150g)
- skim milk- 3/4 cup (150g)
- salt - 1 1/4 tsp (1.42g)
- instant yeast - 1 Tbsp (15g)
- Water- 1/2 cup (125ml)
- large egg, lightly beaten- 1
- agave nectar, separated - 5 tsp (25ml)
- extra virgin olive oil - 4 tbsp (56g)
- poppy seeds- 1 Tbsp (15g)
- cider vinegar - 1/2 tsp (2.84g)

Preparation:

1. Combine the potato starch, xanthan gum, sea salt, sorghum, buckwheat, and millet in a bowl.
2. In a measuring cup made of glass, mix the milk and water. Between 110°F and 120°F should be reached before adding the yeast and 2 tsp (8.4g) of agave nectar. For a few minutes, cover and set aside.
3. Combine the yeast and milk mixture with the olive oil, vinegar, last of the agave, and egg in a new mixing dish. Put wet ingredients in the bottom of the breadmaker.
4. Add the dry ingredients on top.
5. Press Start after selecting the gluten-free cycle and light colored crust.
6. Poppy seeds should be sprinkled after the second kneading cycle.
7. Pan from bread machine removed. After about 5 minutes, remove the loaf from the pan and let it cool on a rack.
8. Enjoy!

Nutritional facts:

Calories: 153, Fat: 5g, Carbs: 24g, Protein: 3g, Sugar: 1g, Potassium: 98mg, Sodium: 292mg

17.4 Gluten-free Cinnamon Raisin Bread

Preparation Time: *5 minutes*

Cook Time: 3 hours

Servings: *12 slices*

Ingredients:

- almond milk- 3/4 cup (150ml)
- warm water- 6 tbsp (90ml)
- flax meal - 2 Tbsp (30g)
- butter - 2 Tbsp (30g)
- apple cider vinegar- 1 1/2 tsp (8.4g)
- brown rice flour- 1 2/3 cup (227g)s
- honey - 1 1/2 Tbsp (45g)
- potato starch- 2 Tbsp (30g)
- corn starch - 1/4 cup (21g)
- cinnamon - 1 Tbsp (15g)
- xanthan gum - 1 1/2 tsp (8.4g)
- active dry yeast - 1 tsp (5g)
- salt - 1/2 tsp (2.84g)
- raisins - 1/2 cup (100g)

Preparation:

1. Flax and water are combined, then leave to stand for five minutes.
2. In another bowl, combine the dry ingredients; leave out the yeast.
3. Fill the bread machine with the wet ingredients.
4. After creating a hole in the middle, add the dry ingredients on top.
5. Add yeast to the well.
6. Select Light Crust Color, Gluten Free, and click Start.
7. Add raisins after the initial rising and kneading cycle.
8. After baking, remove from the oven and place on a cooling rack.

Nutritional facts:

Calories: 192, Fat: 4g, Carbs: 38g, Protein: 2.7g, Sugar: 3g, Potassium: 76mg, Sodium: 289mg

17.5 Gluten-free Pizza Crust

Preparation Time: *5 minutes*

Cook Time: 2 hours

Servings: *8 slices*

Ingredients:

- xanthan gum - 3 tsp (15g)
- potato starch- 1/2 cup (100g)
- cornstarch, 1 cup (130g) and extra for dusting
- Yeast- 2 Tbsp (30g)
- rice flour- 2 cups (240g)
- Milk- 1 cup (130ml)
- Water- 1/2 cup (125ml)
- olive oil - 1/2 cup (125ml)
- Sugar- 1/2 cup (100g)
- large eggs, room temperature - 3
- salt - 1 tsp (5g)

Preparation:

1. Pour the wet ingredients, which have been combined in a different container, into the bread machine pan.
2. Add the dry ingredients to the pan after combining all but the yeast.
3. The middle of the dry ingredients should include the yeast.
4. Select the Dough cycle, then hit Start.
5. Once the dough is prepared, form it into a pizza by pressing it out onto a surface that has been lightly dusted with corn starch. Use this dough with your preferred pizza recipe and toppings!

Nutritional facts:

Calories: 463, Fat: 8g, Carbs: 79g, Protein: 7g, Sugar: 6g, Potassium: 134mg, Sodium: 689mg

17.6 Gluten-free Brown Bread

Preparation Time: *5 minutes*
Cook Time: 3 hours

Servings: *12 slices*

Ingredients:

- large eggs, lightly beaten- 2
- canola oil- 3 Tbsp (42g)
- warm water - 1 3/4 cup (230g)
- oat flour - 3/4 cup (150g)
- brown rice flour - 1 cup (130g)
- potato starch- 1 1/4 cup (260g)
- tapioca starch - 1/4 cup (21g)
- brown sugar- 2 Tbsp (30g)
- Salt- 1 1/2 tsp (6.4g)
- nonfat dry milk powder- 1/2 cup (100g)
- gluten-free flaxseed meal - 2 Tbsp (30g)
- psyllium, whole husks - 3 Tbsp (42g)
- xanthan gum - 2 1/2 tsp (8.4g)
- gluten-free yeast for bread machines- 2 1/2 tsp (8.4g)

Preparation:

1. The bread machine pan should contain the eggs, water, and canola oil. Stir everything together.
2. In a sizable mixing basin, combine all of the dry ingredients with the exception of the yeast.
3. Over the wet components, layer the dry ingredients.
4. The yeast should be placed in the center of the dry ingredients.
5. Press Start after setting the gluten-free cycle and medium crust color.
6. Lay the pan on its side to cool when the bread has finished baking before slicing it to serve.

Nutritional facts:

Calories: 201, Fat: 5g, Carbs: 35g, Protein: 5g, Sugar: 4g, Potassium: 99mg, Sodium: 390mg

17.7 Sorghum Bread Recipe

Preparation Time: *5 minutes*
Cook Time: 3 hours

Servings: *12 slices*

Ingredients:

- salt - 1/2 tsp (2.84g)
- Sugar- 3 Tbsp (42g)
- xanthan gum - 1 tsp (5g)
- guar gum - 1 tsp (5g)
- tapioca starch - 1 cup (130g)
- brown or white sweet rice flour- 1/2 cup (100g)
- sorghum flour - 1 1/2 cup (340g)
- eggs (room temperature, lightly beaten) – 3
- instant yeast - 2 1/4 tsp (1.42g)
- Vinegar- 1 1/2 tsp (6.4g)
- oil - 1/4 cup (21g)
- *Warm* milk - ¾ -1 cup (177ml-130ml)

Preparation:

1. In a mixing bowl, combine all of the dry ingredients excluding the yeast.
2. In the bread machine pan, layer the dry ingredients on top of the wet ingredients.
3. The yeast should be placed in the center of the dry ingredients.
4. Light crust color, Basic bread cycle selected, and Start button.
5. Before serving, take it out and place it on a wire rack to cool on its side.

Nutritional facts:

Calories: 169, Fat: 6g, Carbs: 25g, Protein: 3g, Sugar: 4g, Potassium: 67mg, Sodium: 151mg

17.8 Gluten-free Simple Sandwich Bread

Preparation Time: *5 minutes*
Cook Time: 1 hour

Servings: *12 slices*

Ingredients:

- sorghum flour- 1 1/2 cup (340g)
- gluten-free millet flour or gluten-free oat flour - 1/2 cup (100g)
- tapioca starch or potato starch (not potato flour!)- 1 cup (130g)
- fine sea salt- 1 1/4 tsp (1.42g)
- xanthan gum - 2 tsp (8.4g)
- warm water - 1 1/4 cup (260ml)
- gluten-free yeast for bread machines - 2 1/2 tsp (8.4g)
- honey or raw agave nectar - 1 Tbsp (15g)
- extra virgin olive oil - 3 Tbsp (42g)
- organic free-range eggs, beaten- 2
- mild rice vinegar or lemon juice - 1/2 tsp (2.84ml)

Preparation:

1. Whisk together all of the dry ingredients in a basin, excluding the yeast.
2. Pour the liquid ingredients into the bread machine pan first, then carefully pour the combined dry ingredients on top of the liquid.
3. The middle of the dry ingredients should include the yeast.
4. Click Start after choosing Rapid, 1 hour and 20 minutes, and a medium crust color.
5. Leave to cool for 15 minutes before slicing.

Nutritional facts: Calories: 137, Fat: 4g, Carbs: 22g, Protein: 2g, Sugar: 3g, Potassium: 49mg, Sodium: 85mg

17.9 Gluten-free Crusty Boule Bread

Preparation Time: *5 minutes*
Cook Time: 3 hours

Servings: *12 slices*

Ingredients:

- gluten-free flour mix- 3 1/4 cup (400g)
- kosher salt - 1 1/2 tsp (6.4g)
- active dry yeast- 1 Tbsp (15g)
- warm water - 1 1/3 cup (333ml)
- guar gum - 1 Tbsp (15g)
- olive oil - 2 Tbsp (30ml) , plus 2 tsp (8ml)
- large eggs, room temperature- 2
- Honey- 1 Tbsp (15g)

Preparation:

1. In a sizable mixing bowl, combine all of the dry ingredients with the exception of the yeast; set aside.
2. In another mixing dish, stir the water, eggs, oil, and honey together.
3. Fill the bread machine with the wet ingredients.
4. Over the wet components, layer the dry ingredients.
5. The yeast should be placed in the center of the dry ingredients.
6. Press Start after selecting the Gluten-Free setting.
7. Take the baked bread out and let it totally cool. To use as a boule, hollow it out and fill it with soup or dip; then, slice it to serve.

Nutritional facts:

Calories: 480, Fat: 3g, Carbs: 78g, Protein: 2g, Sugar: 7g, Potassium: 27mg, Sodium: 356mg

17.10 Gluten-Free Raisin Bread

Preparation Time: *5 minutes*
Cook Time: 1 hour

Servings: *12 slices*

Ingredients:

- warm water - 300ml (1 ¼ cups)
- honey - 2 Tbsp (30g)
- olive oil - 60ml (¼ cups)
- apple cider vinegar - 1 Tbsp (15g)
- egg whites - 2
- dry active yeast- 7g (2 tsp)
- granulated sugar- 2 Tbsp (30g)
- baking powder - 1/2 tsp (2.84g)
- gluten-free almond flour / or any other gluten-free flour, levelled - 200g (2 cups)
- Xanthan Gum - 2 tsp (8.4g)
- Tapioca/potato starch, levelled - 100g (1 cup)
- ground cinnamon - 1 tsp (5g)
- salt - 1 tsp (5g)
- raisins - 150g (1 cup)

Preparation:

1. According to your bread machine manufacturer, place all the ingredients into the bread machine's greased pan except raisins.
2. Select basic cycle / standard cycle/bake / quick bread / sweet bread setting
3. then choose crust color either medium or Light and press start to bake bread.
4. In the last kneading cycle, check the dough
5. it should be wet but thick, not like traditional bread dough. If the dough is too wet, put more flour, 1 Tbsp at a time, or until dough slightly firm.
6. Five minutes before the dough-kneading cycle is over, add the raisins.
7. Remove the baked bread from the pan and let it cool on a wire rack after the cycle is complete and the machine has shut off.

Nutritional facts:

Calories: 89, Fat: 1g, Carbs: 12g, Protein: 6g, Sugar: 1g, Potassium: 27mg, Sodium: 10mg

17.11 Gluten-free Sourdough Bread

Preparation Time: *5 minutes*
Cook Time: 3 hours

Servings: *12 slices*

Ingredients:

- Water- 1 cup (100ml)
- ricotta cheese- 3/4 cup (150g)
- eggs - 3
- vegetable oil- 1/4 cup (21g)
- honey - 1/4 cup (21g)
- gluten-free sourdough starter- 3/4 cup (150g)
- cider vinegar - 1 tsp (5g)
- potato starch - 2/3 cup (227g)
- white rice flour - 2 cups (240g)
- dry milk powder - 1/2 cup (100g)
- tapioca flour - 1/3 cup (113g)
- salt - 1 1/2 tsp (6.4g)
- xanthan gum - 3 1/2 tsp (12.4g)

Preparation:

1. Pour the wet ingredients into the bread machine pan after mixing them.
2. Combine the dry ingredients in a sizable mixing bowl, and then pour the mixture over the wet components.

3. Select the Gluten-Free cycle and press Start.
4. After removing the pan from the oven, give the bread within around 10 minutes to cool.
5. Before slicing, transfer to a cooling rack.

Nutritional facts:

Calories: 299, Fat: 7g, Carbs: 46g, Protein: 5g, Sugar: 4g, Potassium: 79mg, Sodium: 327mg

17.12 Grain-free Chia Bread

Preparation Time: *5 minutes*
Cook Time: 3 hours

Servings: *12 slices*

Ingredients:

- warm water - 1 cup (100ml)
- olive oil- 1/4 cup (21g)
- large organic eggs, room temperature- 3
- gluten-free chia seeds, ground to flour - 1 cup (130g)
- apple cider vinegar- 1 Tbsp (15g)
- potato starch- 1/2 cup (100g)
- almond meal flour - 1 cup (130g)
- millet flour - 3/4 cup (150g)
- coconut flour - 1/4 cup (21g)
- salt - 1 1/2 tsp (6.4g)
- xanthan gum- 1 Tbsp (15g)
- nonfat dry milk- 3 Tbsp (42g)
- sugar - 2 Tbsp (30g)
- instant yeast- 6 tsp

Preparation:

1. Add the wet ingredients to the bread machine pan after whisking them together.

2. Add the dry ingredients, minus the yeast, to the wet ingredients after whisking them together.
3. Add yeast after making a hole in the dry ingredients.
4. Press Start after selecting the Whole Wheat cycle and light crust color.
5. Prior to serving, let the bread totally cool.

Nutritional facts:

Calories: 375, Fat: 18g, Carbs: 42g, Protein: 12g, Sugar: 6g, Potassium: 78mg, Sodium: 462mg

17.13 Easy Gluten-free, Dairy-free Bread

Preparation Time: *5 minutes*
Cook Time: 2 hours 10 minutes

Servings: *12 slices*

Ingredients:

- apple cider vinegar - 1 1/2 Tbsp (22g)
- Sugar- 2 tsp (8.4g)
- active dry yeast - 2 tsp (8.4g)
- egg white, room temperature- 1
- eggs, room temperature - 2
- olive oil - 4 1/2 Tbsp (75g)
- warm water - 1 1/2 cup (320ml)
- multi-purpose gluten-free flour- 3 1/3 cup (360g)

Preparation:

1. In a sizable mixing bowl, combine the warm water, sugar, and yeast; stir to combine. Set aside for 8 to 10 minutes, or until frothy.
2. In a different mixing dish, whisk together the two eggs and one egg

white before adding to the bread machine baking pan.

3. To the baking pan, add oil and apple cider vinegar. Baking pan with frothy yeast/water mixture added.

4. On top, sprinkle the all-purpose gluten-free flour.

5. Start with the gluten-free bread setting.

6. Take out the bread from the baking pan, and invert it onto a cooling rack. Before slicing to serve, let the bread cool fully.

Nutritional facts:

Calories: 241, Fat: 6g, Carbs: 41g, Protein: 4g, Sugar: 2g, Potassium: 89mg, Sodium: 164mg

17.14 Cheese & Herb Bread

Preparation Time: *5 minutes*
Cook Time: 1 hour

Servings: *12 slices*

Ingredients:

- dried basil - ¾ tsp (3.7g)
- dried oregano - ¾ tsp (3.7g)
- warm water - 300ml (1 ¼ cups)
- egg whites – 2
- grated Parmesan cheese- 2 Tbsp (30g)
- olive oil - 60ml (¼ cups)
- dried marjoram- 1 tsp (5g)
- Xanthan Gum - 2 tsp (8.4g)
- Salt- 1 tsp (5g)
- baking powder- 1/2 tsp (2.84g)
- gluten-free almond flour / or any other gluten-free flour, levelled - 200g (2 cups)
- apple cider vinegar- 1 Tbsp (15g)
- granulated sugar - 2 Tbsp (30g)
- dry active yeast- 7g (2 tsp)
- Tapioca/potato starch, levelled - 100g (1 cup)

Preparation:

1. According to your bread machine manufacturer, place all the ingredients into the bread machine's greased pan, and select a basic cycle / standard cycle/bake / quick bread / white bread setting. Then choose crust color, either medium or light, and press start to bake bread.

2. In the last kneading cycle, check the dough

3. it should be wet but thick, not like traditional bread dough. If the dough is too wet, put more flour, 1 Tbsp at a time, or until dough slightly firm.

4. When the cycle is finished and the machine turns off, remove baked bread from pan and cool on wire rack.

Nutritional facts:

Calories: 150, Fat: 3g, Carbs: 9g, Protein: 4g, Sugar: 2g, Potassium: 76mg, Sodium: 415mg

17.15 Gluten-free Oat & Honey Bread

Preparation Time: *5 minutes*
Cook Time: 3 hours

Servings: *12 slices*

Ingredients:

- warm water - 1 1/4 cup (295ml)
- eggs – 2
- honey - 3 Tbsp (42g)
- gluten-free oats - 1 1/4 cup (260g)
- butter, melted - 3 Tbsp (42g)
- potato starch- 1/2 cup (100g)
- brown rice flour- 1 1/4 cup (260g)
- sugar - 1 1/2 tsp (6.4g)
- xanthan gum- 2 tsp (8.4g)
- active dry yeast - 1 1/2 Tbsp (22g)
- salt - 3/4 tsp

Preparation:

1. Except for the yeast, add the ingredients in the above-mentioned order.
2. The yeast should be placed in the center of the dry ingredients.
3. Press Start after selecting the gluten-free cycle and a light crust color.
4. Before cutting the bread to serve, remove it from the oven and let it cool for 20 minutes on a cooling rack.

Nutritional facts:

Calories: 151, Fat: 4g, Carbs: 27g, Protein: 6g, Sugar: 2g, Potassium: 67mg, Sodium: 265mg

17.16 Gluten-free Potato Bread

Preparation Time: *5 minutes*
Cook Time: 3 hours

Servings: *12 slices*

Ingredients:

- medium russet potato, baked, 1 or mashed leftovers
- honey - 3 Tbsp (42g)
- gluten-free quick yeast - 2 packets
- eggs,2
- warm almond milk- 3/4 cup (150ml)
- egg white - 1
- tapioca flour- 3/4 cup (150g)
- almond flour- 3 2/3 cup (467g)
- dried chives - 1 tsp (5g)
- sea salt- 1 tsp (5g)
- olive oil - 1/4 cup (21g)
- apple cider vinegar - 1 Tbsp (15g)

Preparation:

1. In a sizable mixing bowl, combine all of the dry ingredients with the exception of the yeast; set aside.
2. In a different mixing bowl, combine the honey, apple cider, oil, eggs and milk.
3. Fill the bread machine with the wet ingredients.
4. Over the wet components, layer the dry ingredients.
5. Add the yeast to the dry ingredients after making a well in them.
6. Press Start while selecting the gluten-free bread setting and a light crust color.
7. Prior to slicing, let it cool completely.

Nutritional facts:

Calories: 232, Fat: 13g, Carbs: 17g, Protein: 4g, Sugar: 3g, Potassium: 67mg, Sodium: 173mg

18 CONVERSION TABLE

Measuring Equivalent Chart

3 tsp (15g)	1 Tbsp (15g)
2 Tbsp (30g)	1 ounce
4 tbsp (56g)	¼ cups (59g)
8 tbsp	½ cup (100g)
16 tbsp	1 cup (130g)
2 cups (240g)	1 pint
4 cups (544g)	1 quart
4 quarts	1 gallon

Type	Imperial	Imperial	Metric
Weight	1 dry ounce		28g
	1 pound	16 dry ounces	0.45 kg
Volume	1 tsp (5g)		5 ml
	1 dessert spoon	2 tsp (8.4g)	10 ml
	1 Tbsp (15g)	3 tsp (15g)	15 ml
	1 Australian tbsp	4 tsp	20 ml
	1 fluid ounce	2 Tbsp (30g)	30 ml
	1 cup (130g)	16 tbsp	240 ml
	1 cup (130g)	8 fluid ounces	240 ml
	1 pint	2 cups (240g)	470 ml
	1 quart	2 pints	0.95 l
	1 gallon	4 quarts	3.8 l
Length	1 inch		2.54 cm

* Numbers are rounded to the closest equivalent

Gluten-Free – Conversion Tables

All-Purpose Flour	Rice Flour	Potato Starch	Tapioca	Xanthan Gum
½ cup (100g)	1/3 cup (113g)	2 Tbsp (30g)	1 Tbsp (15g)	¼ tsp (8.4g)
1 cup (130g)	½ cup (100g)	3 Tbsp (42g)	1 Tbsp (15g)	1/2 tsp (2.84g)
¼ cups (59g)	¾ cup (150g)	1/3 cup (113g)	3 Tbsp (42g)	2/3 tsp (15g)
1 ½ cup (100g)	1 cup (130g)	5 Tbsp (70g)	3 Tbsp (42g)	2/3 tsp (15g)
1 ¾ cup (150g)	1 ¼ cups (59g)	5 Tbsp (70g)	3 Tbsp (42g)	1 tsp (5g)
2 cups (240g)	1 ½ cup (100g)	1/3 cup (113g)	1/3 cup (113g)	1 tsp (5g)
2 ½ cup (354g)	1 ½ cup (100g)	½ cup (100g)	¼ cups (59g)	1 1/8 tsp
2 2/3 cup (227g)s	2 cups (240g)	½ cup (100g)	¼ cups (59g)	1 ¼ tsp (8.4g)
3 cups (360g)	2 cups (240g)	2/3 cup (227g)	1/3 cup (113g)	1 ½ cup (100g)

Flour: quantity and weight

Flour Amount (cup)	Flour Amount (grams)
1	140
3/4	105
1/2	70
1/4	35

Sugar: quantity and weight

Sugar Amount (cup)	SugarFlour Amount (grams)
1	200
3/4	150
2/3	135
1/2	100
1/3	70
1/4	50

Powdered Sugar Amount (cup)	Powdered SugarFlour Amount (grams)
1	160
3/4	120
1/2	80
1/4	40

Cream: quantity and weight

Cream Amount (cup)	Cream Amount (ml)	Cream Amount (grams)
1	250	235
3/4	188	175
1/2	125	115
1/4	63	60
1 tbsp.	15	15

Butter: quantity and weight

Butter Amount)
1 cup (130g) = 8 ounces = 2 sticks = 16 tbsp =230 grams
1/2 cup (100g) = 4 ounces = 1 stick = 8 tbsp = 115 grams
¼ cups (59g) = 2 ounces = ½ stick = 4 tbsp (56g)= 58 grams

Oven Temperature Equivalent Chart

Fahrenheit (°F)	Celsius(°C)	Gas Mark
220	100	
225	110	1/4
250	120	1/2
275	140	1
300	150	2
325	160	3
350	180	4
375	190	5
400	200	6
425	220	7
450	230	8
475	250	9
500	260	

* Celsius (°C) = T (°F)-32] * 5/9

**Fahrenheit (°F) = T (°C) * 9/5 + 32

*** Numbers are rounded to the closest equivalent

19 CONCLUSION

This book has presented you to some of the easiest and delicious bread recipes you can find. One of the most mutual struggles for anyone following the diet is that they have to cut out so many of the foods they love, like sugary foods and starchy bread products. This book helps you overcome both those issues.

Focus your mindset toward the positive. Through a diet, you can help prevent diabetes, heart diseases, and respiratory problems. If you already feel pain from any of these, a diet under a doctor's supervision can greatly improve your condition. These loaves of bread are made using the normal Ingredients you can find locally, so there's no need to have to order anything or have to go to any specialty stores for any of them. With these pieces of bread, you can enjoy the same meals you used to enjoy but stay on track with your diet as much as you want. Lose the weight you want to lose, feel great, and still get to indulge in that piping hot piece of bread now and then. Spread on your favorite topping, and your bread craving will be satisfied. Moreover, we have learned that the bread machine is a vital tool to have in our kitchen. It is not that hard to put into use. All you need to learn is how it functions and what its features are. You also need to use it more often to learn the dos and don'ts of using the machine. The bread machine comes with a set of instructions that you must learn from the manual to use it the right way. There is a certain way of loading the Ingredients that must be followed, and the instructions vary according to the make and the model. So, when you first get a machine, sit down and learn the manual from start to finish; this allows you to put it to good use and get better results. The manual will tell you what to put in it, as well as the correct settings to use, according to the different ingredients and the type of bread you want to produce. Having a bread machine in your kitchen makes life easy. Whether you are a professional baker or a home cook, this appliance will help you get the best bread texture and flavors with minimum effort. Bread making is an art, and it takes extra care and special technique to deal with a specific type of flour and bread machine that enables you to do so even when you are not a professional. In this book, we have discussed all bread machines and how we can put them to good use. Basic information about flour and yeast is also discussed to give all the beginners an idea of how to deal with the major ingredients of bread and what variety to use to get a particular type of bread. And finally, some delicious bread recipes were shared so that you can try them at home!

BONUS: Scanning the following QR code will take you to a web page where you can access 9 fantastic bonuses after leaving your email and an honest review of my book on Amazon: 4 mobile app about bread machine recipes, 1 mobile app to calculate your daily caloric needs and 4 online courses about bread machine. LINK: https://BookHip.com/TCCGLWH

Printed in Great Britain
by Amazon

18390918R00054